UnBranding

UnBranding

100 Branding Lessons for the Age of Disruption

Scott Stratten & Alison Stratten

WILEY

For general information about our other products and services, please contact our Customer Care Department within the United States at (800) 762-2974, outside the United States at (317) 572-3993 or fax (317) 572-4002.

Wiley publishes in a variety of print and electronic formats and by print-on-demand. Some material included with standard print versions of this book may not be included in e-books or in print-on-demand. If this book refers to media such as a CD or DVD that is not included in the version you purchased, you may download this material at http://booksupport.wiley.com. For more information about Wiley products, visit www.wiley.com.

ISBN 978-1-119-41701-9 (cloth)
ISBN 978-1-119-41700-2 (ePDF)
ISBN 978-1-119-41705-7 (ePub)

Printed in the United States of America

10 9 8 7 6 5 4 3 2 1

Contents

The Usual UnIntroduction

WE'VE RECEIVED SOME FLACK OVER the years for our often random and rambling intros on the *UnPodcast*. It seems as though some people would like us to just get to the point.

Well, a few months ago Scott had a weekend gig in the Bahamas, a keynote for a great crowd of franchisees. While Alison usually can't travel with Scott (someone has to keep the children and pets alive), she's no fool—and so she flew out for a couple days to join him in the sunshine. The hotel was glorious, right on the ocean, and as a treat we booked moonlight oceanside massages. It should have been everything—but it was terrible. We each spent the entire time waiting for it to be over so as not to ruin it for the other. The wind was cold, people were walking by, and the massage itself could only be described as irritating. When it was over we just looked at one another and then spent the next two hours laughing about how we are the only two people on the planet who could hate a Bahamian oceanside massage.

We swore never to tell anyone. What kind of horrible people would?

Now we could talk about branding here, find the symbolic nature of the story: everything to make a great brand experience ruined by a number of controllable factors. We could teach a branding lesson. But instead we're just going to leave this here as a confession and an homage to our intro haters.

UnBranding has been in the works for a while now. When you've written *UnMarketing* and *UnSelling*, it seems like the next logical step. But we've always fought against content for content's sake, and we waited until we had something to say. We could tell you how to be a brand in one sentence—be good to your customers, employees, and vendors and have a great product and/or service. But we can't sell that for $20. The message of *UnBranding* isn't new for us. Branding is in every part of your business— how and whom you hire is branding, your front line is branding, what your CEO likes on Facebook is branding. Branding isn't a department or a campaign; in fact, branding isn't in your hands at all. Your brand belongs to your customers—it's what they think of when they hear your name and how they tell your story.

Today, technological innovations and increased access to information have transformed that story. They have disrupted all our traditional relationships: how we hire, market, and even date as well as how we find our favorite foods, watch our favorite movies and television shows, and learn about the world around us. They have changed the dynamic between brands and their markets and between students and their teachers. Our digital age has put a world of information and connection in our hands, and the way we market and are marketed to has changed forever.

The concept of disruption isn't new. It was introduced in 1942 by Joseph Schumpeter, when he wrote about "creative destruction," a concept that described how new technologies, products, and processes make their predecessors obsolete and reinvent businesses, industries, and the economy.[1] While the economic process of the new taking the place of the old may not be revolutionary, the pace at which innovation happens today is. This is the age of disruption.

To be in business today means that one interaction at a local restaurant can change the face of a global brand. Customer service, once an exercise done one-on-one, now happens in public. The online world has blurred with real life, making them one and the same. Today, we learn the truth

---

[1] https://medium.com/singularityu/the-age-of-disruption-7ef2960b0f35#.1x9pxkjv4

about unethical businesses practices with ease, while at the same time those seeking to deceive continually have new tools for doing so. It's enough to make your head spin.

Now before you throw away your phone and run off to book your own oceanside massage, we're here to tell you the truth. The age of disruption means nothing at all. Good business is still good business. While news of your ethical practices or lack thereof may travel further and faster today, what makes them good has never changed. We've always put forward only what we feel is the best version of ourselves; Facebook didn't invent that. "Disruption" means no more and no less than any other buzzword, and even the newest, flashiest technologies, those that change our lives from morning until night, won't change why we love the things we do.

In the following pages we're going to look at 100 brand lessons in the age of disruption, taken from thousands of brand case studies we've researched and studied. We'll talk about everything from changes in the workplace to the value of emerging tools and how change, especially fast-paced change, can be daunting. There can be an instinct to protect ourselves, to attempt to lock down content, to blame technology rather than embrace it, to focus on the overall change rather than making real improvements to our core values and practices. We're going to fight that instinct together and see innovation as an opportunity. We're going to look at companies, big and small, that have navigated innovation and change both successfully and not so successfully, to find actionable lessons we can apply to our own branding.

If you want to dig deeper and don't feel like copying out an 85-character URL from the footnotes, visit www.UnBookLinks.com for all the sources included in the book, listed by chapter.

Let's have some fun and get through these crazy times together, one brand lesson at a time.

The Moral of the Brand Story

OVER THE YEARS WE'VE READ hundreds, if not thousands, of brand stories. We do this so you don't have to, fine reader, because it's our job and because we absolutely love them. We're fascinated by what makes businesses thrive, grow, and sometimes self-destruct. From all these stories we've distilled the four factors of brand loyalty, factors that ensure you will thrive in the face of disruption and innovation and that, given your focus, will lead to success.

A note on success before we continue. In many of the companies we look at, success has been a victim of innovation as well. As individuals we are faced with countless versions of it, and we need to remember to decide for ourselves how it will be measured and experienced. Financial success to us means having a home we are proud of; having the ability to provide safety, comfort, and opportunities for those we love; and having a little extra on the side to leave in Las Vegas a few times a year. For you, it may mean being able to quit your current job to pursue a dream, attend college, independently feed and clothe your family, or buy the car you've always wanted (or buy any car for that matter). Business success for us means maintaining the status quo—a life where we get to do the things we dreamed of doing, where Scott gets to be onstage, and we can have people like you read (and hopefully enjoy) our work. For you, business success may be seeing your product in a store, reaching the Fortune 500, partnering with people you respect, or getting that raise you've been hoping for.

As we caution you about chasing the "next big thing" in business and in digital, we also caution about chasing other people's ideals of success. We're here to tell you that you don't need to be working toward someone else's definition of the next big achievement. It's okay to answer the question of "what's next for me?" with "I'm going to keep enjoying what I have now."

And that ends the self-help section of *UnBranding* :). Now back to loyalty.

We all want loyal customers and to become a habit in someone's life— the golden rewards of being the coffee they always drink, the hotel they always stay at, the accountant they've worked with for years, the store they always go to, and so on. In loyalty we are impermeable to competition, and our business is chosen without any other choice even standing a chance. So how do we create loyalty in the age of disruption? By focusing on four key factors; comfort, cost, convenience, and convergence.

1. *Comfort.* All the successful brands we've seen brought their customers from a feeling of need or want into one of comfort. They focused on answering a question for the market, whether it concerned a product or service. Once the need had been met, customers walked away confident that in the future the company would rise to the occasion again; this way trust was born.

2. *Cost.* Until an innovation comes about where we don't exchange currency for goods and services, cost will always be important. This doesn't mean to create loyalty one should race to the bottom, price-wise; in fact, many of our most habit-forming brands are among the most expensive in their market. Focusing on cost really means focusing on perceived value and giving people what they paid for. Our most successful brands made it their job to ensure that customers felt their money was well spent, to explain why their products are of value, and to keep the price promise.

3. *Convenience*. Products and services don't only cost the customer's money, they also cost time. This factor relates to all your business processes, from the number of hoops people need to jump through on your shopping cart to how far they need to drive to your store. Everyone is busy, and our successful brands earned loyalty by appreciating and saving customers' time.

4. *Convergence*. Loyal customers feel their ideals line up with the companies they work with. The most successful businesses understand their customers and what they believe in, making their products and services part of the individual's identity. There isn't one ideal for everyone, which is why when some people flee from a brand for aligning themselves with something, others flock to it. Our most successful brands have been names people said they were proud to be loyal to.

In the chapters ahead we will look at 100 branding stories in the age of disruption and see how creating loyalty by focusing on comfort, cost, convenience, and convergence has kept them level in the bumpy world of innovation. From established, well-known brands to the corner store, online and off, these businesses all have something we can learn from. From some, we'll learn what to do—and from others, in true *UnMarketing* style, we'll learn what not to do.

Lesson 1

Logos Don't Matter

IF YOU'VE EVER SPENT TIME designing or redesigning a logo for your company, raise your hand. Don't worry, no one in the Starbucks will notice.

Remember the long meetings, going over and over the tiniest details, deciding which blue better represents your mission statement or choosing a font or two. You're never going to get that time in your life back.

We're here to let you in on a little secret: logos don't matter. And they certainly aren't the be-all and end-all of branding. We spend so much time and money on logos, but our brands aren't in our business hands; they belong to our market. Your brand changes with each interaction—a living, breathing relationship between you and the world.

Let's picture two logos. The first is an apple with a bite taken out of it. You can see it, and you may even be holding it in your hand reading this book. When you picture that logo, you'll think of two things: the most recent and the most extreme (good or bad) experience you've had with the company. For us, we think of how great the laptop is we're using to write this chapter (most recent), and about all the times they've replaced Alison's phone, no matter where she dropped it (most extreme).

The second logo we want you to picture is a circle, within which you'll find a V and a W. When you see it, you may picture the car you drove to Starbucks in, and you may also remember how the company it belongs to was outed for deceiving its market and polluting the environment on a global scale. The smog doesn't even need to be added to the lettering.

That's branding, and you'll notice it had nothing to do with apples or cleverly shaped letters. If the bite was moved to the other side or the color was changed, our brand understanding would remain the same. We love logos because they can be controlled and pushed out, but branding in the age of disruption cannot be.

Our logo lesson from Apple and Volkswagen is that a logo needs to be clear and concise and it shouldn't offend. It should be designed by designers, not by a group of people who can't even get an appropriate outfit together. A logo should be consistent so that it reminds people of the good business you're investing your time and money into providing. You can't redesign it to fix your problems, and you shouldn't try. Instead, focus on the stories behind the logo—create current positive experiences and long-lasting "*wow*"s to delight and move your market into comfort and loyalty.

Lesson 2

Peanut Butter Branding

OUR HOUSE IS VERY POPULAR with UPS, and FedEx, and those Amazon delivery folks. Our online ordering addiction aside, people send us stuff. Over the years, we've been sent shoes, doughnuts, Google Cardboard (Alison didn't know what it was until the 13-year-old freaked out and showed her how it worked), a ton of books, and even a knife set. But none of this has ever impressed our children—that is, until the box of peanut butter showed up. After we met him at the National Speaker's Association annual event, Clint Greenleaf (co-founder and CEO of HomePlate Peanut Butter) finally gave us the street cred with our children that has so far eluded us.

Clint and his pro-athlete partners had seen baseball players eating peanut butter, an inexpensive, heat-stable, high-calorie snack, the way college kids ate ramen noodles. They saw a need in the market for healthy peanut butter that didn't separate in the jar, tasted as good as the high-sugar varieties, and was all-natural and no-stir—and HomePlate was born. Using the quality of and need for the product, along with their connections to professional baseball, Clint and his partners got HomePlate into club-houses, and players loved it.

When news of a story about basketball players crossed the HomePlate desk—specifically about the Golden State Warriors not being able to get their favorite PB&J sandwiches to the court—HomePlate was sent to the rescue. When Steph Curry[1] says he loves your product, what else do you need? Here is a great example of active listening and action, creating amazing branding opportunities.

Today HomePlate is still a small company of about six employees, with products in grocery and retail locations in the United States. They handle feedback quickly and deal with negative feedback by the "approach of solving the problem first, and saving face second." Clint believes customer service is a critical part of HomePlate's marketing. He loves the flexibility that being a small company allows and told us, "when you're all sitting in the same room, you can develop a plan for how to deal with customer service consistently. Branding is easier when you're smaller because we're all on the same page."

Homeplate also gives back to its community. Twelve-year-old Bella Grace Parker[2] (BG to her friends) has been playing softball since she was three and dreams of one day playing in the Olympics. However, after years of suffering stomach aches every time she ate, BG was diagnosed with Crohn's disease. To manage the disease, she had to make radical adjustments to her diet. Her mom began searching for options to keep her healthy, maintain her weight, and keep her softball dreams alive and found the answer in HomePlate Peanut Butter. BG loved the taste, and the product has all the calories, protein, and nutrients she needs to keep her healthy. BG's mom credits HomePlate with changing their lives for the better. In true HomePlate style, the company visited BG's team and brought enough peanut butter for the girls' entire season.

There are many branding lessons to be learned from Clint and HomePlate Peanut Butter. One of the most powerful for us was the importance of recognizing, valuing, and utilizing your strengths. Clint and his partners knew their market and valued the needs of athletes. They utilized their connections and spread the word (and the peanut butter)

[1] http://homeplatepb.com/tag/steph-curry/
[2] http://www.kvue.com/mb/news/local/peanut-butter-helps-girl-with-crohn-s-disease/440745366

accordingly by putting their product in as many players' hands as possible. They then took this success and realized that a greater market would value it as well. Throughout our conversation with Clint he mentioned strength after strength, defining his business, his partners, his employees, and his customers by what they brought to the table. The challenges of working with food, of being a small company, and even those of depending on endorsements from celebrities were never his focus. Far too often in business we see only our faults and we are left continually on the defensive. Good branding is about bringing value, and that starts with valuing what you bring to the table, or in Clint's case, what you bring to the table and to the dugout.

Lesson 3

We Know You Think You're Good, but Are You GoodWell Good?

Fast Company recently featured a business called GoodWell that offers an audit for your company. This is not the kind of financial audit we're used to that brings to mind tax evasion and frozen bank accounts (not us personally—what have you heard?). This audit rates your business practices. While most companies claim to be good places to work, few are. Issues of pay discrepancy and a general lack of communication and training are the norm, and these issues travel down the line to the customer, creating poor experiences. GoodWell looks at 11 indicators, ranging from current employee satisfaction to the attrition rate. It collects the data and rates businesses, nonprofits, and even governments, providing a type of social seal of approval where "rather than just being profitable and fiscally responsible, they can earn a certification as a fair, equitable, and humane place to work."[1]

---

[1] https://www.fastcompany.com/40410840/would-your-company-pass-this-stringent-good-workplace-audit

As we'll see throughout *UnBranding*, the age of disruption has created a digital megaphone for all things good and bad in your company. We can no longer focus on keeping issues quiet; rather, we are now forced to change. It's one of our favorite things about social media: when you treat your employees and/or your customers poorly, the world finds out. With this increase of access to information, consumers who care about buying from good companies can make educated choices. Good business equals good branding.

Here are the 11 factors GoodWell looks at in its audits.[2] We ask you to consider each one and think about how your business would rate.

1. As an employee, how likely are you on a scale of 1 to 10 to recommend working at your company to others?
2. What is the ratio between the salary of your highest-paid employee and of your average employee? (To pass the GoodWell audit, the ratio cannot be higher than 100. So if Scott makes $1,000 per year, the cats can't make less than $10 a year on average.)
3. What is the ratio between your executive team's average salary and the average salary of your employees? (See the previous example, but now average in Alison's salary and include the dogs with the cats.)
4. What is the ratio between the average male employee's salary and the average female's salary in similar jobs?
5. What is the ratio between the average salary of any population segment (visible minorities, for example) and the average salary for similar jobs?
6. What is the total number of injuries on the job?
7. What is the percentage of underage workers?
8. What is the percentage of part-time workers?
9. What is the percentage of workers making below-poverty-line wages?
10. What is the attrition rate?
11. What is the percentage of employees participating in the benefits package?

Valued, respected employees stay in their jobs. They communicate better as teams and provide optimal service to customers. The challenge is

---

[2] http://www.goodwellworld.com/the-metrics/

to make employees feel valued and respected, and we think GoodWell's rubric offers the perfect place to start. Our GoodWell lesson is that it isn't enough to focus on earnings when evaluating your company's success, nor is it effective to wait until market share starts dropping to turn your eyes inward for solutions. If you want to improve your bottom line, you need to improve your front line, and the best way to do that is with critical business analysis and hard work.

Lesson 4

Selling Cookies Is a Dirty Job

LEADING UP TO EMMA'S[1] MARKETING United Conference this past year, we ran a contest on the *UnPodcast*, giving away two trips to Nashville, conference passes, and as an added bonus (and if the winners wanted to, of course), dinner with us. Two of the winners were amazing women from Kellogg's, and we thoroughly enjoyed meeting them and sharing some Peg Leg Porker BBQ together. As a surprise, because they'd listened to our *UnPodcast* episode where we spoke about Mike Rowe and Girl Guide Cookies and because Kellogg's makes the treats, they brought us a box of every single flavor. Scott was in heaven, and we brought all the cookies home for a taste test with the kids to see which was their favorite. The Thin Mints won in a landslide. We had tons of fun tasting the cookies and especially loved having the kids guess their names. Really, all food should have names like Do-Si-Dos or Savannah Smiles.

If you have kids and have the pleasure of cooking for them, you know they cannot tell a lie. Unlike adults, most of whom will muscle through a

---

[1] Emma is the sponsor of the *UnPodcast*.

meal they don't love out of kindness, kids will actually flat-out refuse to eat—or possibly worse, spit out food they don't like. Full-on grimaces, torture-like cries, accusations of poisoning—these are not uncommon sightings when testing out a new recipe. Scott would eat a meal he didn't care for without a complaint for the next 30 years if Alison cooked it for him. The children wouldn't last 30 seconds.

Back in January, Mike Rowe, the celebrity known for his TV show *Dirty Jobs* and his all-around awesome support for trades and tradespeople, posted a video about Girl Guide Cookies. Before we watched it, Girl Guide Cookies weren't really on our radar. None of our kids were in Guides and other than Scott's buying a bunch of cookies every season, we'd never paid much attention to the brand. The video is hysterical; Mr. Rowe himself breaks down laughing every few moments, and it really shouldn't be missed. There's a link in footnote 2 of this chapter if you want to check it out. Go ahead, watch it now. We'll wait[2].

In the video, Mr. Rowe reads a letter sent to him by Sean McCourt, who works with him on his podcast. The letter is an email sent by Mr. McCourt's 11-year-old daughter Charlotte to one of her dad's friends from high school, one who her dad told her is very rich. In the letter, Charlotte asks Mr. Rich Friend to consider buying some Girl Guide cookies from her. To help him choose which ones, she rates the cookies—on a scale of 1 to 10—with all the honesty of an 11-year-old.

The perennial favorite Thin Mint (as our children would agree) earned a 9 for its "inspired" combination of chocolate and mint. The Do-Si-Dos peanut butter sandwich cookie earned a 5 for "its unoriginality and its blandness," while the Savannah Smiles earned a 7 for its "divine taste." "If you have a wild sense of adventure, try the S'mores," Charlotte wrote of this year's new s'mores-inspired cookies. "Full disclosure, I have not tried the S'mores so I cannot rate it in good conscience." Charlotte's least favorite is Toffee-tastic, which she called a "bleak, flavorless, gluten-free wasteland" and added, "I'm telling you, it's as flavorless as dirt."

A bleak, flavorless, gluten-free wasteland. We love Charlotte so much. We just hope she never switches her focus to rating business books.

---

[2] https://www.facebook.com/TheRealMikeRowe/videos/1417382278271911/

She didn't give any of the cookies a rating of 10; as she explained, "There's a reason for this. It's because the only way to get a 10 is by donating a box—any box. It helps strike a spark into the treacherous lives of those men and women protecting our country and keeping America safe."

We also hope she doesn't decide to start writing business books, because we honestly cannot compete with that quality of writing.

As Mr. Rowe says in the video, Charlotte understands one of the fundamental tenants of sales—"you can't sell a product unless people first trust you. And the best way to get people to trust you is to tell them the truth." Charlotte's goal was to sell 300 boxes of cookies; she ended up selling 26,086 boxes and 12,430 were donated to the troops. Our lesson here is that honesty matters. Tell the truth in your marketing and advertising, be honest in your business practices, build trust with your employees and vendors, and good things will happen. As Mr. Rowe wrote on his site, "[There are] many reasons to feel good about this story, but my personal favorite is still the fact that Americans are standing by to reward honesty and decency wherever and whenever it appears. Thanks to everyone on this page for playing along."

We couldn't have said it better ourselves.

Lesson 5

Complacency and ADT's Lame Season's Greetings

OVER THE YEARS, WE'VE RAILED against creating content for content's sake. Forcing yourself into a calendar can lead to a lot of bad content, made and shared only because of what day it is. A lame post on Mother's Day isn't good simply because of what day it is, and no one has ever shared your company's newsletter because you sent it out on Wednesday. We understand the value of planning your content along with the inspiration holidays and events can bring, but if the quality isn't there, you're just conditioning your audience not to care.

Perhaps the worst example of putting in the least effort possible that we've seen was from ADT Canada, who released a video (we use this term with hesitation) in its December newsletter.[1] The moving picture was no more than a letter from the firm's president, Andrea Martin. She didn't read the letter, mind you, and she didn't even do a voice-over. The written

---

[1] https://youtu.be/-0cS7zo5ROU

letter just scrolled along the page with music playing in the background, and it didn't even scroll in a cool, opening of *Star Wars* kind of way.

There are a number of things ADT could have done instead:

1. Create an actual video of Ms. Martin wishing customers a happy holiday. People love video, right?
2. Don't want to be on camera? Read the letter! Shake things up a bit, and use images of actual people at the company rather than scrolling text.
3. Skip the video, and send the letter as text (you know, because it *is* text).
4. Skip the whole thing. Reach out to customers only when you actually have something of value to share.

Our branding lesson from ADT is not to let your brand get lazy. Maybe ADT is a great company with a wonderful product that enriches people's lives. Maybe a lame video will in no way change that or how someone who is actually in the market for their services would make their choices. Lameness is unlikely to cause the end of your company, but that doesn't mean you can or should just mail things in because you can usually get away with it. While this may not be earth-shattering stuff, it is a perfect lesson in treating opportunities to connect with your customers with care rather than laziness.

The bigger issue here is that laziness breeds complacency, and complacency is the enemy of business success. It opens doors to our competitors, increases the chances of mistakes missing our radar, and reflects poorly on our brand in general and specifically on our products and services. No one wants to hire a complacent security company, and the lack of focus and effort in one area of ADT's business affects the brand as a whole. When we're just starting out, we tend to be driven and detail oriented, but once we've found success we can sometimes become lazy. Look for ways to keep yourself driven, don't forget your competition, and remember that your customers deserve effort in all your brand interactions.

Lesson 6

Pizza Saves Lives

BECOMING A HABIT IS THE ultimate goal in building customer loyalty. Just ask the café you always stop at for coffee in the morning or the local pet-food store you drop into on your way home from work every other Tuesday. Habit feeds community. You get to know the owner, the other customers, and your fellow entrepreneurs working at the local coffee shop. Our parents were great at this. Alison's mom can tell you all about the bookstore clerk with the best recommendations and the Tim Horton's employee who has her coffee ready before she orders. Habit brings value both to the business and the customer. It's one of the things the online world works hard to mimic from brick and mortar.

Our favorite example of habit this year came from Domino's Pizza. You probably have a place you always order from. Next time you do, think about how "that place" became "the place" for you and remember our four loyalty factors (comfort, cost, convenience, and convergence). We always order from Gino's Pizza whenever our friend and contractor extraordinaire Jay comes over. The kids love Jay, but they also know that Jay's car in the driveway means pizza for dinner. Jay = Pizza = Fun.

When workers at an Oregon Domino's realized that a regular customer with health concerns had an irregular time between his orders, the staff were concerned.[1] They decided to take action and sent out a delivery person to check on him. "When the driver arrived, he saw lights on and heard the TV, but no one answered the door and the phone went straight to voicemail. He called for help, and when paramedics arrived, they found the customer lying on the ground in his house. It's believed he had a stroke, but it's not clear when he was affected."

They saved his life. The manager even visited him in the hospital, saying, "'I think we were just doing our job checking in on someone we know who orders a lot. We felt like we needed to do something.'"

That kind of concern for customers and for other humans is something we could all show more of. This is much more than a branding lesson; it's a lesson on how we should all care about others. Nurturing habit is about nurturing community. and that can't and shouldn't be a campaign—it should be a way of life.

---

[1] https://consumerist.com/2016/05/10/dominos-workers-come-to-customers-rescue-after-noticing-he-hadnt-ordered-pizza-recently/

Lesson 7

The Diet That Crossed the Line

A FEW YEARS AGO, ALISON stopped buying gossip magazines. To be fair and so as not to seem as though this was a moral decision on her part, she did so under some duress from Scott. He felt, and rightly so, that they make money off other people's suffering, promote unhealthy lifestyles, and generally set a less-than-optimal ideal of beauty. Since Alison couldn't argue with any of these points and gets more than enough celebrity gossip from Instagram, she stopped buying them.

Magazine brands like *Cosmopolitan* are synonymous with celebrity break-ups and fad diets. That's their brand, and it's up to us to decide if that's what we're into. So when a recent issue featured the article "How This Woman Lost 44 Pounds Without Any Exercise,"[1] it could easily be passed off as the norm. The thing is, this woman didn't lose weight eating only celery, or potatoes, or purple foods between 11:00 AM and 2:00 PM; this woman lost weight because she had cancer.

---

[1] http://pagesix.com/2017/04/11/cosmos-new-weight-loss-tip-get-cancer/

The article explained that when the 31-year-old woman was diagnosed with a severe kidney infection, doctors discovered a malignant carcinoid tumor of the appendix. She underwent multiple surgeries and suffered horrible complications. "After she was diagnosed with 'post-traumatic stress disorder' triggered by her cancer diagnosis, she turned to food, later losing weight on a diet called The Bod." She could not exercise; the article explained that "she's still recovering from surgery, she isn't physically able to work out the way she used to before her cancer diagnosis."[2]

Safe to say, this is not the way anyone would ever want to lose weight. Social media agreed, slamming the magazine and demanding a change. *Cosmo* kept the article, but it did change the title to "A Serious Health Scare Helped Me Love My Body More Than Ever."

Clearly, there is a line, and *Cosmo* found it. Readers will happily accept unfounded gossip about strangers, revel in stories of failure and deceit, take in 101 sex tips, and accept that if they ate only chives they too could lose that post-baby weight. But they won't accept cancer as a diet plan. Our lesson here is to know your line as a brand. Don't act in the name of looking edgy to get attention, because some kinds of attention are things we could all do without.

[2] Ibid.

Lesson 8

Leadership in Action

IN THE AGE OF DISRUPTION, leadership is more important than ever. Companies that are successful in navigating digital innovations have strong leadership guiding the way.

- *Leaders make decisions that guide practice.* These often involve tough choices and run counter to the "what we've always done" mentality.
- *Leaders take these decisions and create action.* When decisions live only in mission statements and directives without action, brands suffer. In fact, they suffer more with the incongruence between mission and practice than they would otherwise.
- *Leaders take responsibility.* When things go wrong, a true leader is out in front taking responsibility. They don't shift blame, they don't throw vendors and employees under the bus.
- *Leaders lead in their actions, not just in their words.* Leading by example is an art, a continuous process, and the key to true leadership.

For us, there is no better example of leadership than the founder of Patagonia, Yvon Chouinard. Patagonia is a 40-year-old American company that manufactures and sells outdoor clothing. Mr. Chouinard started out making pitons (metal spikes used in climbing) because the ones available at the time were for one-time use only. He taught himself blacksmithing and made pitons that could be reused in order to diminish waste and leave mountains as untouched as possible. His pitons became popular and his company grew, diversifying into other gear. By 1970, Chouinard Equipment had become the largest supplier of climbing hardware in the United States.

As the industry leader, he ended up having to make a tough call when the climbing world changed and his gear went from being seen as environmentally friendly and reusable to being considered an environmental villain. Climbing had become more popular and was concentrated into a few popular routes. With the same cracks having to endure repeated use of pitons, the damage was severe. Although this was not his intent starting out, Chouinard saw the damage and decided to phase out of the piton business. He acted out of his concern for the environment, even though the change was a huge business risk. Rather than defend his original stance, shift the blame, or ignore the problem, he acted, not only on paper but with decisive real-world action.

As with the pitons, Chouinard saw another hole in the outdoor market: there were no colorful, fashionable clothes for men. On a winter climbing trip to Scotland in 1970, Chouinard bought a rugby shirt to wear while rock climbing. Back in the States, Chouinard wore it around his climbing friends, who asked where they could get one, and his clothing company was born. He started making the kind of clothing he and his friends wanted—of good quality, durable, and fashionable. The company grew at a rapid rate until the summer of 1991, when sales fell during a recession. To pay off the company's debt, management had to drastically cut costs and inventory and lay off 20% of the work force. This was a tough time for the company, and it taught Chouinard a major lesson. The company has purposely kept growth modest ever since—another tough business decision.

Since 1984 Patagonia has had no private offices, an office arrangement that can create distractions but also keeps communication open. The company has a cafeteria serving healthy, mostly vegetarian food and an on-site child-care center (one of only 150 in the country when it started) and offers flexible work hours and job sharing. Chouinard himself takes months off every year, months during which he is unreachable. "People know if the warehouse is on fire, not to call me. What can I do about it?"[1] He credits this and the success of the company's flexibility on hiring energetic, independent workers who are encouraged to take time off to surf, to spend time with their families, and to make their own hours.

Patagonia runs national environmental and educational campaigns. From early on, the company took a stand against globalization of trade whenever it could compromise Patagonia's environmental and work standards. We've never seen a company site with Patagonia's level of transparency around manufacturing, including factory photos, details, and a global map of where all products are made, from material sourcing to manufacturing. Every year and a half it holds a Tools for Activists conference to teach marketing and publicity skills to the advocacy groups it works with. In 1996, all its cotton fabric was moved to organic cotton, and it actively continues the search for more environmentally friendly fabrics.

Perhaps Patagonia's most important value is quality. While its clothing is expensive and well-made, it is also repairable, creating high perceived value. Rather than encouraging customers to buy new products, Patagonia provides repair guides so people can get as much use out of their clothes as possible. Customers can send in damaged clothing for free repairs or recycling. This spring, for the third year in a row, Patagonia's Worn Wear College Tour visited campuses around the country. Students could bring garments, regardless of brand, in for repair—in a vintage wooden camper truck, of course.

Patagonia's values aren't only good for the environment, they're good business. As with current trends in food, shoppers are placing a higher value on where their clothing comes from and how it's made. They will spend 10% to 15% more on ethically produced clothing, according to Marshal Cohen, retail analyst at NPD Group. "The younger generation, in particular, is willing to pay for the responsibility factor, because they're not buying as much stuff in the first place," Cohen said. "Th things that are good for the environment and are going

[1] http://www.npr.org/podcasts/510313/how-i-built-this
[2] http://www.adweek.com/brand-marketing/consumers-care-about-sustainabl and-these-brands-are-providing-it/

Alison's grandmother always told her to have fewer clothes but they should be of high quality; we aren't sure whether this is a younger-generation value, but either way we love it. When clothes are cheap, they become disposable. Save your money for something that lasts. That's what Grandma wanted, and she lived to be a very wise 99 years old.

Patagonia became the first benefit corporation, back in 2012—a certification and a movement that:

> provides a clear and dependable path for business leaders who believe business can and must be an agent of positive change in our troubled world. Rather than scrambling to respond to daily affronts with little strategy, benefit corporations embed their core values directly into their legal charter. As a result, the company can act purposefully at all stages of decision making, balancing transparency with the need to achieve reasonable financial gain while also taking deliberate action to create additional benefits for multiple stakeholders whenever possible. In other words, benefit corporations take real steps to ensure that business is good for people and good for the planet. The program eliminates the false choice between making money and doing the right thing.[3]

To pass along their success to others, Patagonia recently launched $20 Million & Change, an internal fund to help "like-minded, responsible start-up companies bring about positive benefit to the environment." As Chouinard explained, "Others might see Patagonia Works and $20 Million & Change as revolutionary business ventures; we think both are just next logical steps to doing business more responsibly. Economic growth for the past two centuries has been tied to an ever-spiraling carbon bonfire. Business—and human—success in the next 100 years will have to come from working with nature rather than using it up. That is a necessity not a luxury, as it's seen now in most business quarters. We invite and encourage all companies to start to work with us in that direction."[4]

/www.bcorporation.net

The lessons you can take away from Patagonia are lessons from Chouinard's leadership. Embrace innovations that make sense, keep your values clear, and use them to dictate practice. Make tough choices, take environmental responsibility seriously, and lead by example—from hiring, to workplace design, to setting out expectations and responsibilities. When your values align clearly with your company's activities, you are able to provide the kind of transparency that will set you apart. Success in the age of disruption isn't driven by the bottom line; it's value driven. Chouinard has said that since the recession, he has decided to start making decisions with the assumption that they'd be in business for 100 years, rather than looking quarter to quarter. How would your business actions change if you thought this way?

Lesson 9

Hubris and Using Brands You Hate

ALISON HATES BANANAS, BUT SHE still has to put them in the kids' lunches. She may know them to be Satan's fruit, but the children she loves need healthy lunch options, and if bananas are their choice, then bananas they get. Alison (the company) must listen to the needs and wants (a yellow, vitamin-rich assault on the taste buds) of her kids (the customers), because an eaten banana is better than a wasted apple.

There are times when you need to change your view of a brand because your market dictates that you have to. We see this a lot in our digital age as we adapt to new communication tools. You may hate Twitter or texting your customers, but if your market overwhelmingly chooses that tool, you need to adapt or die. When things are changing around you, you need to change too; it shows respect for your customers, demonstrates an understanding of their needs, and maintains your place as a choice of ease, all factors that create and foster convenience.

Here is an example from one of our Facebook fans.

Erin Blaskie wrote: "Infusionsoft. They used to employ some skeezy marketing tactics, which I hated, but now I have to like them because so many of my clients use them and they are one of the only platforms that does what it does."

If you aren't familiar with Infusionsoft, it is a company that offers customer relationship management software, such as email marketing and other sales products. If you're a business consultant like our friend Erin, then you can't ignore them or what they bring to the table for your customers. Moreover, since her customers are using Infusionsoft, she needs to be able to advise them intelligently, and she can't do so if she chooses to ignore them.

For us, this happened with the iPhone. We were big BlackBerry fans, particularly for the keyboard feature. But as the iPhone dominated the tech conversation more and more, especially at events where Scott was the keynote speaker, he needed to be able to speak about the iPhone's innovations and apps. He couldn't do this without using the technology himself.

The lesson here for our B2B readers is that whether it's Apple or a banana, your market dictates which brands you need to understand and use. The answer to why you won't adopt something can't be "because I don't like them." Hubris, "the characteristic of excessive confidence or arrogance, which leads a person to believe that he or she may do no wrong,"[1] is extremely dangerous in business, particularly in today's innovative times. While the same characteristic is often what allows entrepreneurs to get started in the first place and gives individuals the confidence to go after the positions they want, that confidence can come back to bite us when it blinds us to new ideas and to working well with others. The key is to remain self-assured while keeping an open mind about the needs and wants of our market.

---

[1] http://www.investopedia.com/terms/h/hubris.asp

Lesson 10

Creepy Disruption

JUST BECAUSE WE CAN DO something doesn't always mean we should.

Living in a time of fast-paced innovation means that sometimes our ability to create is incongruent with our human ability to accept or function within a new framework. That's the reason it's so important to ask ourselves "why" before using new technology—not only to avoid spending resources on something that may or may not lead to business success but because sometimes the innovation is ahead of our markets' learning curve. Or, as in the case that follows, just plain creepy.

In 2017, ads for Disney's new *Beauty and the Beast* movie were hard to miss. While most of us saw them in familiar places—magazines, posters, in previews for other family movies—Google Home customers were served up the promotions in a new and "innovative way".[1] The ads were played unexpectedly by Google Assistants through the Google Home unit. For example, when the Assistant said good morning, along with giving requested information about weather and traffic, people online were told about the new movie:

---

[1] http://bgr.com/2017/03/17/google-home-audio-ads-beauty-and-the-beast/

"By the way, Disney's live-action *Beauty and the Beast* opens today," Google Assistant said. "In this version of the story, Belle is the inventor instead of Maurice. That rings truer if you ask me. For some more movie fun, ask me something about Belle."

So. Very. Creepy.

Users hadn't asked for the latest in film openings in their area. They weren't given the information while asking for movie listing times and locations. It was simply served up.

When confronted with customers displeased by the ads, Google responded first by saying the ads weren't ads at all: "This isn't an ad; the beauty in the Assistant is that it invites our partners to be our guest and share their tales." Even the company reply sounds like an ad from *Beauty and the Beast*! Now that's product placement! In the end, the feature was removed. It seemed that although people were ready for the Home service, they weren't into getting beastly ads with their morning updates.

We're going to talk a lot about the value of collecting and using data properly in *UnBranding*, but back in 2012, Target took an innovative approach to data collection a little too far. One of their statisticians, Andrew Pole, had figured out a way to use collected data based on purchase history, to figure out if a customer was pregnant. Target targeting pregnant women was good for business—the company could send out coupons and promotions for baby projects, and help to build brand loyalty during a time when customers tend to be buying a lot of new products and breaking old purchase habits. New parents "are exhausted and overwhelmed and their shopping patterns and brand loyalties are up for grabs."[2] Companies know this, and target new parents from the moment a baby is born. If Target was able to reach them during pregnancy, they'd have a jump on the competition.

Mr. Pole developed a program that was able to take shopping data from customers and identify "about 25 products that, when analyzed together, allowed him to assign each shopper a 'pregnancy prediction' score. More important, he could also estimate her due date to within a small window, so Target could send coupons timed to very specific stages of her pregnancy."[3]

---

[2] http://www.nytimes.com/2012/02/19/magazine/shopping-habits.html

[3] Ibid.

Seems harmless enough, right? Except there's one tiny detail missing—whether or not the women in question has told her family that she's pregnant—as was the case when an angry father walked into a Target with a set of pregnancy-focused coupons that had been sent to his teenage daughter.[4] He demanded to speak to the manager and accused the store of encouraging his child to get pregnant. After a heated exchange, the father spoke to his daughter, who was indeed pregnant, and later apologized to the manager for his anger.

Digital innovations have led to countless changes in all our lives, and sometimes adapting to these changes can be challenging. We accept that Facebook and other platforms will know what sites we've been looking at, and target relative ads. We expect people to have phones in their pockets, and demand attention accordingly. We go to parties and events knowing photos may end up online. These are all things we've gotten used to, and now expect—but it didn't happen overnight, it took time. While we may not be ready to hear ads through our Google Home speakers, we do embrace asking questions into an inanimate object and then having the object talk back. Our lesson here is that as times change—make sure you aren't getting ahead of your market with technology they aren't ready for.

---

[4] http://www.businessinsider.com/the-incredible-story-of-how-target-exposed-a-teen-girls-pregnancy-2012-2

Lesson 11

That Time We Newsjacked

FOR YEARS WE'VE FOUGHT AGAINST the practice of using tragic news events as ~~inspiration springboards~~ clickbait to encourage your audience to open your content. We find the practice lazy at best and in poor taste. When a public figure dies, when there's an emergency or catastrophe, your job as a brand is to express condolences, offer help, or shut up. Because the popularity of a term takes it up to the top of searches, like the top-stories feature on Twitter for example, many brands will use that term in their headlines, leading people to see and then click on their content.

When a television show is at its peak, we see stories like "What *Breaking Bad* Can Teach Us about Investing" or "Seven Management Lessons from *The Walking Dead*." When Gene Wilder died, we saw articles about "How to Manage Like Willie Wonka" like the one on page 30.

And every day (seriously) we are sent screenshots like the one on the following page from the Gap.

Gross. Using others' suffering, even when it's very popular suffering, in your marketing is bad for business. Period.

What If You Managed Like Willy Wonka?
Gene Wilder's passing reminds us of his famous Charlie and the Chocolate Factory.

We understand using a calendar to manage content. We get that holidays like Valentine's Day and Halloween can shape what we write about, and more important, what people are going to be looking for. However, the content needs to be there first. It needs to be good to bring value, and we believe it needs to be kind. After those three factors have been met, look at your calendar.

The thing is, this year, we newsjacked, something we promised ourselves we'd never do. When a story hit the news about a man being violently dragged off a United Airlines flight (something we'll be talking about more in the "United We Fall" chapter), we didn't just share the story, we recorded an emergency episode of the *UnPodcast* and shared it that day. It was one of our most popular episodes. Did we feel we had something good, valuable, and kind to add to the conversation? Yes. Did we want to be front and center in the conversation? Yes. Did we get listens because of a man's suffering? Yes. And we aren't so proud of that last part. For us, the lesson here was about absolutes in business. Maybe jumping on a news story isn't a good practice, but for us in this instance, we felt it was beneficial to our audience and to our business. You will have to make tough decisions like these every day, so please decide carefully where you'll fall.

Lesson 12

Guacamole Is Extra, but Using Your Image Is Free of Charge

OFTEN, WE BARELY EVEN NOTICE them. As we sit in a restaurant or food court, the photos on the walls kind of blend into the background, don't they? They consist of images of overly happy people enjoying food and conversation, perfectly prepared versions of whatever burger we're having, and painted landscapes to create the Italian or French theme. They're all painstakingly created and chosen by the owners and designers who created the restaurant, along with its menu and logo.

Imagine for a moment what you would do if one day while out for burgers or burritos you looked up at the wall beside you and saw your own face, smiling back at you. Now imagine that rather than this being a modeling gig you'd brag to your friends about, you didn't okay this whole picture-on-the-wall thing. In fact, you can remember once being in the restaurant and having your picture taken, then refusing to sign a release that would have allowed the company to use it. We imagine you'd be pretty angry.

Well, one California woman who saw her face in Chipotle did just that—she got angry. She saw herself on their walls without having given her permission, and she sued the restaurant for $2.2 billion. After the photo was taken back in 2006, the photographer had approached the woman and asked her permission to use it in their marketing material, and she refused to sign the release. The photographer offered the photos to Chipotle, who did not bother to check for a release and went ahead and used the photo but not before editing it to change the woman's hair and add beer bottles to the scene. The woman claimed that by adding the drinks "Chipotle put a false light upon her character associated with consuming alcoholic beverages."[1]

Ethical marketing practices are critical to good business. We see far too many people every day blurring the lines of what's right and what's wrong, all in the name of selling their product. Some use the images of famous people and celebrities or their words without permission and proper compensation. We beg you to source quotations and properly compensate people for their images. It takes years to build a company and an ethical brand people trust, and just one stolen image can tarnish that good name. Our lesson from the Chipotle example is that the age of disruption doesn't offer any tools to repair broken ethics or change how valuable they are. The restaurant should have ensured that the images were being used with permission. Your ethics quota isn't refreshed once a quarter, and your customer's trust is not a renewable resource.

[1] https://consumerist.com/2017/01/09/woman-sues-chipotle-for-2-2-billion-over-a-photograph/

Lesson 13

The Kidz Are Alright

WHEN WE WERE YOUNG, THEY were called the Minipops, and we loved them endlessly. Alison spent hours listening, choreographing dance routines, and singing along. Who wouldn't love all the fun of popular songs, without bad language, sung an octave higher on repeat? Her mom, that's who. Alison really owes her a lengthy apology.

Many entrepreneurs who are just getting started are looking for a niche—some part of the market that's been untapped. We start companies to fill needs and answer questions we find left unanswered and to bring our market from a feeling of need or want into one of comfort. We can imagine that kid-appropriate versions of popular music was such a product for parents whose kids wanted the songs without the language. Sometimes entrepreneurs learn quickly that what they saw as a need was less of one than expected. The niche was too small or too difficult to reach to build a successful company. Other times, the need and want for your niche product is much, much larger than anyone could have expected—even us.

When we read an article in *Music Business Worldwide* discussing the Kidz Bop launch in the UK, it included a statistic that really surprised us.

Kidz Bop creates and sells the modern-day version of the Minipops, and in 2015 it accounted for 23% of all children's music sale in the United States. That is a tremendous amount of sales. "The best-selling series has had 24 Top 10 debuts on the Billboard 200 Chart. Only three artists in history—the Beatles, the Rolling Stones, and Barbra Streisand—have had more Top 10 albums."[1]

Those are numbers any musician would be incredibly proud of. Beyoncé hopes for those numbers. They have live concerts, streaming and purchase options in a number of formats, an app on LeapFrog, a Sirius FM radio station, and branded toothbrushes that play their music. An important branding lesson for all of us is the enviable number of ways Kidz Bop has created for customers to conveniently consume their music and connect as a community—all kid-focused and parent-friendly, just like their music.

---

[1] http://www.musicbusinessworldwide.com/razor-ties-kidz-pop-brand-expands-into-uk-with-universal/

Lesson 14

Online Theft and Why It Should Matter to You—Yes, Even You

IMITATION IS THE SINCEREST FORM of flattery, they say. Well, a man named Charles Caleb Colton actually said it, although we've seen it credited to Oscar Wilde as well. Who knows who said what, right? In this case, being misquoted may be the ultimate in irony; you can quote us on that.

We see quotations used without credit every day, on social media, in advertising materials, and spoken from stages. We've had our own words and work taken and used without credit. We beg you not to do this; it makes you look lazy and underhanded and degrades the value of creative work in general. Imitation is not the sincerest form of flattery; giving credit is. Content theft is just a quick hop, skip, and jump away from stealing others' ideas and designs. The digital age has given us all access to so much information—access that has resulted in a lot of inspiration and imitation—and laws protecting creators have been slow to catch up.

In 2016, clothing chain Zara was accused of stealing ideas from 12 different artists. One artist in particular, Tuesday Bassen, filed an official complaint with the company. The 27-year-old illustrator, who has previously worked with brands like Urban Outfitters and Nike, accused Zara of appropriating four pieces of her original artwork without permission or compensation. Fans of her work noticed a similarity between Zara's designs and hers (seen below) and shared their concerns with Bassen.

Zara replied, claiming that the designs were not similar enough to justify action and that the number of complaints they'd received was insignificant compared with the amount of traffic to their site.[1] Basically, because Zara is a huge, popular company and Bessen is a lesser-known artist, the complaints don't count.

This is nothing more than business bullying, and it needs to stop. It cannot be acceptable to steal from artists simply because you have a larger platform. As one of our UnMarketing Facebook fans, Michaela Alexis, wrote when asked about a brand that had changed in her mind, "ZARA. I don't necessarily HATE them now, but it used to be my go to. Two things happened. One, I watched *The True Cost* and became more educated about the impact of fast fashion, and then they totally unapologetically started ripping off artists. As a creative person, I can't possibly support a company that cares so little about human beings and the planet." If you'd like to learn more or get involved, artists launched a site called ShopArtTheft .com, where they are uniting artists, providing resources for those who feel their work is being copied, and sharing media stories from around the world written on the topic.

Maybe you've never written any words that could be stolen. Maybe you aren't an artist or designer looking to ensure ownership of your work. Maybe you think online theft won't affect you and all this stuff really should be seen as a compliment. Well, we'd bet that you probably do share photos online—of your food maybe or even of your children. Now imagine those photos were taken and used in an advertising campaign without your permission and without compensation. That's exactly what happened to our good friend Danielle Smith.

A Facebook friend of Danielle's, who was living in the Czech Republic, sent her a message one day that read:

Alright, so how's this for random: I'm in the car, taking my wife for a checkup, pass by a new grocery store and notice that they have a picture of you, your husband, and two kids on the store-front window. Life size. I kid you not. Will take a photo of it later today and send.[2]

[1] http://fortune.com/2016/07/20/zara-stealing-designs/

[2] http://www.extraordinarymommy.com/stolen-picture/

Photo credit: Danielle Smith

Danielle was shocked. She hadn't given permission for the photo to be used, and no one had approached her to try to get it. When she shared her story, she received some of the most hateful messages we've ever encountered, blaming Danielle for putting images of her family online in the first place, calling her naive for posting high-quality images, and even going as far as to comment on the attractiveness of her children and husband. Danielle was much stronger and kinder in the face of these comments than we would have been, and we admire her for that. She did nothing wrong. She was the victim of some company a world away that didn't care or think anyone she knew would notice the ads.

After the story blew up, the Associated Press was able to find the store owner who was using the image. He claimed a designer he'd hired made the decision to use the photo and removed it from their site. Danielle wrote a post that included tips for anyone looking to prevent this type of thing from happening to them and has given us permission to share these with you.

If you would like it to be impossible for someone to steal your photos,

1. Don't post any online.
2. Purchase software that disables right-clicking.
3. Use a site like TinEye.com. They are a reverse photo-search website where you can check whether anyone is using your images without permission.

Here's what not to do:

1. For that particular picture, in addition to it being posted on her site, she posted it on another social networking site—a Ning site (a site that allows a group of like-minded people to gather, connect, and exchange ideas). She didn't realize that this site was not secure; that fact was in the fine print, but she didn't realize it.
2. She posted the photo in high resolution, making it easy for the company to blow it up.
3. She labeled the photo "This is my happy family," which is ideal for search engine optimization. But this is how the shop in Prague found it; they Googled "happy family," and guess who popped up, right from the nonsecure Ning site.

We're so grateful to Danielle for sharing her story and to artists like Tuesday Bassen for standing up for their art. We need to hear them, to support them, and to stand up against online theft. Our lesson for brands is this: things on the Internet are not free for the taking. People who would never dream of breaking into Danielle's home to raid her photo album, who would never have the nerve to photocopy artists' designs at an art show, seem perfectly comfortable with right-clicking and doing their worst. It's a new world, and innovation makes theft easier, but behind every image, every design, every song, and every word there is a person—a person whose work deserves the same value and permission we deem legal and use responsibly in real life.

Lesson 15

Confessions of an Old Grumpy Guy

No, THIS IS NOT THE beginning of Scott's autobiography.

Digiday.com publishes a cool series called "Confessions,"[1] where they do anonymous interviews with someone in a specific industry related to marketing. The articles are always great to read, and we love them. Recently, one featuring a financial-industry firm's chief marketing officer caught our eye.

Scott has been the keynote speaker at a bunch of financial-industry conferences, and we've found the industry offers a few unique issues, particularly connected with digital innovation and social media.

For one thing, the issue of security is always front and center. People's livelihoods and savings are not something to manage lightly, especially online, where information can be shared, stolen, and/or misused. As we speak about innovation in a positive light, it's always important to remember that the same fast-paced improvements we can use for good also carry inherent risks.

---

[1] https://digiday.com/series/the-confessions/

Second, the financial industry deals with a number of constraints around privacy of information and rules governing "financial advice"—with whom it can be shared and the responsibilities of the entity sharing it as well as government regulations concerning information and insider trading. We've found that along with these real constraints come perceived ones as well, given that most people on social platforms aren't talking about this level of detailed information. Rather, they're sharing cat videos and talking about their kids. Social media is less about personal financial information sharing and advice and more about generally building awareness and trust.

One of the lessons we can learn from those in the financial industry who are creating community and building trust online is how to manage real constraints while still benefiting from digital innovations. As we mentioned, the majority of online conversations amount to passive conversations about universal things. We connect over the day-to-day stuff that makes us all human: parenting, traffic, how we're treated as customers, coffee, wine, and what we had for lunch. We don't build community sharing the new financial app we're selling.

Anyway, our anonymous financial CMO gave us lots to think about.

Q: What's the biggest mistake people are making in the marketing industry now?

A: I think that the people in their schools—mostly with their MBAs—have been taught this whole idea of disruption in advertising. It's done to such a degree that they don't realize that marketing is not about disrupting people's lives. It's about engaging them within a social or cultural phenomenon. The thing people get wrong is that someone actually cares about your brand.

Semantics! I'm not sure we're both talking about the same thing when we say "disruption." We don't mean interruption; the entire premise of UnMarketing began by turning away from marketing to people the way they hate to be marketed to. To us, disruptive marketing isn't the equivalent of a cold call received at dinner time; it's about new ways of reaching our customers that change or disrupt the way we market in general.

When asked about financial companies using social media, Captain Anonymous had this to say:

Q: Isn't it about *fear of missing out* (FOMO) for those of you who weren't texting with teenagers six years ago or weren't on SnapChat inside these organizations?

A: Yeah. My CEO said to me "we need a Facebook page" years ago. And it's because his daughter said so. I kept asking why. Social is a fraud. There are so many frauds. The biggest one these days is people who do social media or "listening." One guy stopped talking to me because I asked him why we'd pay for something we can get for free. There is a lot of bullshit, but people don't recognize it.

At this point in the interview, we realized that it's entirely possible this person is just grumpy about change. He goes on to refer to people in his company as "young people." We're pretty sure people who speak this way would have been against installing telephones in the office too. Work would be so much easier if we didn't have to "listen," right?

Obviously, we're teasing Grumpy Pants a bit. In many ways we agree that companies do jump into new digital platforms because they fear missing out. Asking why is one of the tenets of UnBranding, and indeed, the premise that social media is the be-all and end-all of marketing is a fraud. Social media is a tool that can be confusing, misused, and to use our CMO's words, "a lot of bullshit." The lesson here, is to make sure that when you're asking why that you turn the question on yourself as well. Because if the answer to "why aren't you open to using new technology to grow your business?" is "because that's not how we did it in my day," you need to reconsider how your bias is framing the conversation.

Lesson 16

Gender Gap

As MANY PARENTS KNOW, FINDING appropriate clothing for kids can be a challenge, especially for those of us lucky enough to be the parents of girls. At best, we find ourselves drowning in a sea of pink and flowers, pocketless, without the rugged qualities needed for a serious day on the playground. At worst, we see sexualized styles and cuts meant for women, shrunken down with inappropriate messaging, like "happy girls are the prettiest," etc.

Our daughters notice, especially those with brothers. It's discriminatory, an early warm-up for misogyny, and it's wrong. To keep our own daughter in clothing on par with her brothers' costs us at least twice, sometimes three times as much. And that's just the financial cost; there's also the time it takes to find these clothes. Why can we go into our local mall and find dozens of options for our science-, or sports-, or superhero-loving sons and nothing for our daughter? Why can our boys have shorts they can climb in and hide lord only knows what in the pockets of, while our girl is left with short-shorts and skinny jeans?

Young Alice Jacob noticed.[1] At five, she was already keenly aware that the clothes she wanted just didn't exist. So with the help of her parents, she wrote the following letter to the Gap.

Dear Gap,

My name is Alice Jacob and I am almost 5½ years old. I like cool shirts like Superman and Batman shirts and race car shirts, too. All your girl shirts are pink and princesses and stuff like that. The boys' shirts are really cool. They have Superman, Batman, rock-and-roll and sports. What about girls who like those things like me, and my friend Olivia?

Can you make some cool girls' shirts please? Or, can you make a no boys or girls' section—only a kids' section?

Thank you,
Alice Jacob

We look forward to Alice being president one day. She has our support.

This letter from a child could have been ignored. The decision to put new designs in stores is a big one, involving design and manufacturing changes months, even years, in the making. We get why a large retailer would need to carefully consider before making restructuring changes (like eliminating gendered shopping sections) that would affect hundreds of locations around the world. These aren't small changes.

The Gap didn't ignore Alice. Instead, it replied:

Hi Alice,

I got hold of the letters you sent in and wanted to be the one to reply to you. I'm Jeff and I'm the head of Gap.

You sound like a really cool kid with a great sense of style.

At GapKids, we try to always offer a wide range of styles and choices for girls and boys. This includes a selection of girls' tees with dinosaurs,

---

[1] https://www.washingtonpost.com/news/parenting/wp/2017/03/06/dear-gap-and-other-retailers-listen-to-this-girl/

firetrucks, sharks, footballs, and some of our superheroes. Our latest Disney Collection, Beauty and the Beast, is also all about the strength and bravery of girls, and that's something that's really important to us.

But, you are right, I think we can do a better job offering even more choices that appeal to everyone. I've talked with our designers and we're going to work on even more fun stuff that I think you'll like.

In the meantime, I'm going to send you a few of my favorite tees from our latest collection. Please check them out and let us know what you think. Our customers' comments are very important to us, and they help us create even better products with each season.

Thank you again,
Jeff
Gap Brand President & CEO

We love the Gap for answering Alice. We love how they listened, acknowledged her concerns, and provided information and both a short-term solution for her and a longer-term promise to do better. The brand value of listening and respecting your customers is immeasurable, especially in a social-media world where customer service like this can be shared publicly. For a business, the branding lesson here is in valuing feedback. We hope other retailers will take a lesson from the Gap, because when Alice is president, all girls will have affordable, accessible options for clothing.

Lesson 17

The Roof Is on Fyre

IT'S A REALLY GOOD IDEA in the world of marketing to have a product or service to sell before focusing on selling it. That might seem obvious to you, but remember common sense isn't so common. A lot of companies get to the point with a new product where they feel awareness is the thing separating them from success. They truly believe that if only they were one of Oprah's favorite things, they'd be millionaires! We saw this a lot when Alison was running her business: dozens of small-product companies thought they were just one celebrity endorsement away from hitting it big.

The thing is, you need to be prepared for success. Otherwise you're better off without the spotlight on you. When the Walmart buyer orders 10,000 pieces, when your site is bogged down because of all the traffic, when your phone won't stop ringing, you need to be ready. Awareness is gold for a solid, quality product. But without the logistics to deliver, the spotlight can be blinding. Just ask the folks who organized and marketed Fyre Festival.

Fyre, which was organized in part by rapper Ja Rule, was sold as a high-end, exclusive music festival with tickets going for between $1,000 and

$125,000. As you'd expect at these prices, this wasn't sold as your run-of-the-mill "thousands of teens in a big open field" concert. Organizers promised gourmet food and accommodations as well as mingling with influencers and models. Marketing utilized celebrity social-media endorsements from famous, bikini-clad figures, such as Kendall Jenner and Bella Hadid.[1]

When the weekend arrived, guests found themselves less than impressed. Rather than goods as advertised, they discovered disorganization. Many customers were stranded without proper transportation and faced long delays. Sewage facilities broke down on the first day and musicians canceled. Rather than gourmet food, they were given two slices of bread and cheese, nothing to drink (let alone alcohol). Promised "eco-friendly, geodesic domes" accommodations ended up being disaster-relief tents. And there weren't even enough of those to go around.[2]

One story, from a Fyre employee, Chloe Gordon, told of a total lack of planning and organization, sub-par accommodations, and a shark-infested beach. Gordon wrote, "Organizers knew that the event would not be up to the standard they had advertised and were advised to postpone the festival until 2018. The decision was overturned when a guy from the marketing team said, 'Let's just do it and be legends, man.'"[3]

There were definitely signs way ahead of time that things weren't going to work out, but the organizers ignored them and kept promoting. Ironically perhaps, the very technology that had allowed the festival to sell tickets was used to share the horror story, with countless social-media accounts sharing photos and tales of disaster from Fyre, all in real time. Legendary, indeed!

As we write, there are currently six lawsuits against Fyre for a variety of issues.[4] One against the founders came from a North Carolina couple who paid $4,600 for a VIP villa at the Bahamas festival. However, like many other ticket buyers, they never even made it to the Exumas, having been

[1] http://nymag.com/thecut/2017/04/fyre-festival-exumas-bahamas-disaster.html
[2] http://www.adweek.com/brand-marketing/in-the-wake-of-fyre-festival-fiasco-will-the-effectiveness-of-celebrity-influencers-take-a-hit/
[3] http://nymag.com/thecut/2017/04/fyre-festival-exumas-bahamas-disaster.html
[4] http://www.rollingstone.com/music/news/fyre-festival-organizers-hit-with-sixth-lawsuit-w481274

stuck at a Miami airport after Fyre shut down following its disastrous first day. Another suit lays blame at the feet of social-media influencers, naming the organizers of the festival as well as 100 influencers that made up Fyre's marketing campaign. One legal battle is over cease-and-desist letters sent out by Fyre to those sharing their personal experiences at the event.[5]

Our lesson here is to make sure you're ready for that spotlight, before paying a Hadid or a Jenner (or whichever sisters are Instagram-famous when you're reading this) for their attention. Product problems and bad service are not what you want to be known for. If they had started small, Fyre might have been able to fix their logistics issues and solve their problems before the world was watching. All new ventures have bugs, but you can decide to fix those on a smaller scale. However, if you get Fyre greedy, those bugs may just end up trending worldwide.

---

[5] http://www.npr.org/sections/therecord/2017/05/03/526758059/a-second-lawsuit-against-fyre-festival-also-targets-its-tribe-of-influencers

Lesson 18

A Cup of Goodwill

THE ONLINE PARENTING COMMUNITY IS pretty awesome. It's actually how we met. Alison was running her maternity and nursing lingerie company, Scott was writing for a popular parenting site, and their online worlds collided. When he tried to check out her company's website from a local coffee shop, he couldn't because it was blocked as porn. And the rest is history.

When dad @GrumpyCarer reached out to his online community for help in finding a discontinued sippy cup for his son Ben[1] he never could have imagined the results. Ben is autistic and would only drink from that cup—otherwise he wouldn't drink at all and would end up in the hospital suffering from dehydration. His father tweeted the picture that follows, asking for people to check their homes for any identical cups and share the search with others.

---

[1] http://www.dailymail.co.uk/femail/article-3983242/Father-s-search-sippy-cup-autistic-son-comes-end.html

Photo credit: Marc Carter

His request ended up being retweeted over 12,000 times.

The manufacturer of the cup heard about the search and decided to help. They searched their warehouses and ended up finding the mold to make the blue Tommee Tippee cup for a special production run just for Ben.

The brand lesson here is always to try and help—however you can. We may not all be able to save the world or give millions of dollars to charity— but we can do what we can.

Lesson 19

Whatever Fake Doesn't Kill You Doesn't Always Make Your Brand Stronger

IN SMALL AND LARGE COMPANIES alike, teams are important. Successful cooperation and collaboration are critical to good branding. The ingredients and environment that make up the ideal team vary as much as the individuals in them. Diversity in experience, age, and background along with supportive and non-judgmental communication and frequency and duration of time spent together all play important roles. On the other hand, when teams fall apart all hell can break loose in a company; work suffers and retention falls. This is why companies invest time and money in team building, which is a big business in its own right. Retreats, exercises, courses, and excursions promise to bring people together and improve creativity and productivity. At UnMarketing we don't need team-building exercises because we have five children to maintain our united front (although we have been known to take a few yearly retreats to Las Vegas).

The big question is whether team-building exercises actually work. The answer is, it depends. If as a manager you're avoiding listening to employee feedback, if communication isn't prioritized and people feel undervalued and powerless, then no amount of rock-climbing trust exercises can help you. If your employees works remotely, a well-timed face-to-face get-together may be all that you need. We've seen companies use large events like South by Southwest (SXSW) as an opportunity for just this kind of team building. We may live and connect online today, but nothing beats in-person meetings for building trust and connection.

If things are running along well with your business and you're looking to optimize your teams, you may seek out some of the popular options for team building. Everything from culinary events to sports-skills training and art can be and are shaped for team building. And if none of these interest you, remember that nothing brings people together like near-death experiences.

Wait, what?

Yes, that's what we said: near-death experiences.

For the so inclined there are companies offering simulated life-threatening scenarios for team building. Survival Systems USA,[1] which teaches survival skills to groups like the F.B.I, the National Guard, and the New York Police Department, offers simulated plane crashes (complete with downwash from rescue helicopters) and generates rain, darkness, 120-mile-per-hour winds, smoke, and fire. The company claims they've seen improved morale and self-esteem from participants, who come away realizing they have skills they never knew they'd had before—skills like not drowning.

Needless to say, we have some concerns. While such experiences may work for some individuals and some teams, their extreme nature could be very stressful for many. Since either non-participation or refusing to go would likely be judged by co-workers and employers, individuals who aren't comfortable with the activity may feel forced to participate, adding further stress, possible trauma, and likely greater dissatisfaction at work. Whatever fake doesn't kill you doesn't always make you stronger.

If you like the danger/challenge aspect but want to do something a little less extreme, you may want to try escape rooms. For our 13-year-old's birthday this year, we went and checked one out, and it was a pretty fun, if

---

[1] https://mobile.nytimes.com/2017/01/07/business/need-better-morale-in-the-workplace-simulate-a-plane-crash.html

Photo credit: George Etheredge/The New York Times/Redux

stressful, experience—and we picked the easiest room the place had. These challenges can be a lot of fun, and if your team is on board they can also be an effective way to learn more about one another[2] and about each others' strengths and challenges in a non-work setting.

If you're thinking about incorporating some team building into your workplace,[3] here are some lessons we've learned.

1. Consider the team and carefully select the kind of activity. Make sure it's inclusive and that all members can participate. For example, if the activity is physically active, make sure all members can be part of the activity.
2. Consider the issues your teams may be facing and whether this type of exercise is the best way to go. If you haven't communicated with team

---

[2] https://roomescapeartist.com/2016/06/26/two-years-of-room-escapes-the-growth-of-the-us-market/
[3] https://mobile.nytimes.com/2017/01/07/business/need-better-morale-in-the-workplace-simulate-a-plane-crash.html

members, you can't possibly know what issues may come up, so do the work before making any plans.

3. Don't walk away from the exercise without follow-up. To get the most from team-building activities you need debriefing. Take the lessons learned and shared and use them to put actionable goals in place for your teams.

Lesson 20

pH Branded for Her

OVER THE YEARS, WE'VE SPOKEN about marketing to women many times. There's the Bic pen for women—because of their dainty hands, of course. There's the car company that told Alison they have women-owners evenings where customers are shown how to "use the radio and other controls," because silly, tiny womens' brains are unable to grasp technology.

We love the idea of companies thinking about their customers as outside the white-male-shaped box. But simply pink-washing your products isn't respecting your audience. Our new favorite example is women's earplugs![1] They're ultra-soft, pink, and other than color, exactly the same as all the other earplugs on the market.

They're not even pH balanced to specifically block out the sounds of children sniffing and chewing.

If you want to appeal to a broad market, perhaps consider what parts of your product they would love and focus on making those better. More comfortable earplugs would appeal to everyone as would manufacturing a variety of sizes so all people can have a comfortable fit rather than just

---

[1] https://www.walgreens.com/store/c/walgreens-women's-earplugs/ID=prod6191617-product

dyeing the tiny ones pink. Gendered marketing is lazy, and for many, offensive enough to make your brand a no-go.

How about a car for women? Or as some companies would call it, a car! When car manufacturer SEAT and *Cosmopolitan* magazine got together to create a gem of a car, the backlash was louder than they could have expected. The vehicle came "complete with jewel-effect rims, a handbag hook, and eyeliner headlights that are emphasized in the same way as make-up emphasizes the eye."

We knew our car was missing something.

The vehicle's "exclusive design and thoughtful feminine touches"— which are the culmination of two years of collaborative research and development—make it perfect for "impromptu karaoke performances, last-minute wardrobe changes, dramatic gossip sessions, and emergency lunch-hour kips," according to the dynamic branding duo.[2]

Two years. Just think of all the good in the world they could have done or of all the real improvements they could have made to actual cars to make them safer and more comfortable.

The branding lesson here is that there's nothing wrong with making your tools in a rainbow of colors, adding purse hooks to your cars, or thinking about how women might use your products. There's nothing wrong with including these factors and innovations in your marketing. Just share them without branding them based on gender and allow your market to choose.

---

[2] http://edition.cnn.com/2016/09/22/autos/cosmopolitan-seat-car/index.html

Lesson 21

Man Cold Marketing

WHEN COMPANIES GROW TIRED OF dyeing things pink and branding them "for women," they can always look to another gender for inspiration—men. Now, we know you may be thinking, "Scott and Alison, isn't *every* day marketing-to-men day?" While it's true that defaulting to pink tools and lady-gentle razors when trying to appeal to women is related to so much focus usually being on men as customers, there are some companies that make it a point to ensure the men in our lives feel extra special. And sadly, they do it with the same misogynistic approach we just read about in our "pH Balanced for Her" chapter.

Our three favorite product culprits are cold medication, cleaning products, and easy-prep food products.

As one of our Facebook fans, Adrian George, shared about the cold medicine Robitussin:

> In this day and age of men not only being equal in helping to raise children but loving being involved, having their marketing always displaying the sick dad as a baby and the household being saved by "Dr Mom" is insulting. I cook, clean, help our children with getting

59

ready for school/homework, etc., and when I'm sick it has to really be a bad one before I might take a half day. It's archaic, and I avoid their products whenever possible now.

Amen to that, Adrian.

That's the thing about gendered marketing—it ends up insulting both men and women by relying on stereotypical roles. Take the personal-grooming products that tell you to "wash like a man, disinfect like a man," all with manly smells and dark, masculine packaging. Food is advertised as being so easy to make even a man can make it, because we all know that one needs dainty lady fingers to whip up some instant pasta.

All of these products should have any number of features that could be focused on in a commercial. Relying on this type of bias is insulting to everyone involved and so very lazy. Just in this past year on the *UnPodcast* we've featured Brogurt, the yogurt for men, man candles with scents like "fart" and "barbeque," and lip balm for men, because clearly Chapstick is a gateway lipstick.

Yes, that's right. We said "Brogurt."[1] We love made-up words on the *UnPodcast*. For this unnecessarily gendered product, we have a double win because it's not only branded to men, it combines Scott's least-favorite man word "bro" with yogurt!

It's served in "man-size" 8-ounce cups (because ladies could never possibly hold or eat that much!) with manly black-and-red packaging, and as the company website put it: "We decided to develop a new Greek yogurt specifically suited to address the unique health and nutrition needs of the most neglected consumers in the category: men." In a totally unscientific poll, we questioned the six people who live in our house and three of them love yogurt (two males, one female) and three hate it with a fiery vengeance (two males, one female). All six agreed the packaging was completely and totally unimportant in this decision.

Our branding lesson here is to focus on the *why* rather than the *who* in your marketing. If your cleaning products are easy to use, sell that. If they have a variety of scents, from musky to floral, sell that. Unless your product specifically targets the genitals, we suggest not bringing them up at all.

---

[1] http://time.com/money/4360406/gender-marketing-products-pen-laundry-yogurt/

Lesson 22

Stop and Thinx

WHEN YOUR PRODUCT FITS APPROPRIATELY into a gender category, as with Thinx panties, using powerful, pro-female messages can be incredibly effective. We first heard about Thinx because of their ads, like the one that follows.

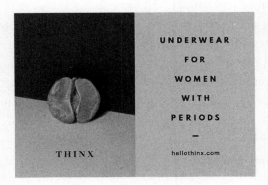

The company featured strong, female-focused marketing, described as a type of backlash to the gendered products we just spoke about, the ones that make us all ranty. The messaging is in line with the product and therefore would be excellent branding. It certainly put them on our radar, along with a lot of other people's. Viewed by many as risky, a similar campaign was almost banned from the New York subway back in 2015. The campaigns were conceived of and created by a team of "young, in-house creatives with no advertising experience, rather than an agency commanding six figures for the project,"[1] and we loved them.

When we learned that Thinx also donated proceeds to help women and girls in developing countries who are unable to attend school "because of lack of access to menstrual supplies and the shame associated with periods"[1] we loved them even more because not only were they creative, they offered us congruence with our values.

What we wouldn't learn until later was that behind the ad campaign was a company in distress. Employees were coming forward with complaints about erratic behavior by the cofounder, little to no health and employment benefits, and sexual-harassment accusations.[2] And so ended the strong feminist message and, therefore, congruency. It's critical to think about branding as a constantly evolving and changing thing. There are no neutral brand interactions; we are constantly moving and reacting with new information and experiences. Your brand is a living, breathing relationship.

Thinx founder and CEO Miki Agrawal, ended up stepping down as CEO and shared her experiences and reasons behind the change.[3] She admitted to making "tons of mistakes" and said she didn't believe she was best suited for the operational CEO role, nor was it her passion to occupy it. She hired a professional CEO and senior-level managers, including a human resources (HR) manager to put appropriate policies in place for employees. She blamed the lack of previous support for employees on fast-paced growth that left her running without HR support for much too long.

Just to be very clear, you cannot and should not blame the presence of sexually-harassing employees on fast-paced growth. We hope those affected found their compensation (and hopefully new, healthy work

[1] http://www.racked.com/2017/3/14/14911228/thinx-miki-agrawal-health-care-branding
[2] http://fortune.com/2017/03/21/thinx-miki-agrawal-sexual-harassment/
[3] https://medium.com/@mikiagrawal/my-thinx-ride-141a738993ee#

environments). We do, however, feel there are many lessons we can learn from Thinx about branding.

1. Gendered messaging can work when it makes sense for your product.
2. Gendered messaging is especially powerful when it's congruent with the culture of your company.
3. The company you start won't have the same needs as the company you grow, and it is your responsibility to assess and keep up with these needs. Your employees can help you with this, if you create an environment where they can communicate safely and effectively.
4. Invest in your business; don't think you can do everything yourself. Outsource your weaknesses, seek experts and advisors, hire people and treat them well.

Lesson 23

Happy Hot Sauce Accidents

"I DON'T BELIEVE IT." SCOTT and Alison, out loud, in unison.

We had just read that Bob Ross, the beloved, afro-rockin', godfather of painting instructions and happy accidents, was never paid a nickel for his legendary show. He did each and every one for free.[1] It blew our minds. The show was created to promote his company's painting supplies. Come to think of it, he was actually one of the first "content marketers" we'd ever experienced, long before digital innovations made the term a marketing buzzword.

The most effective forms of branding happen when we don't realize we're being marketed to. Not in a "neuro linguistic programming" pseudoscience kind of way—rather in an ethical form where the content is so good that we can't wait to take the next step with creators and buy whatever it is they're trying to sell.

Enter FirstWeFeast.com, Complex Media, and their YouTube series. The show first caught our eye with a video featuring Kevin Hart, participating in the show's "Hot Ones Challenge."[2]

---

[1] http://mentalfloss.com/article/23260/5-happy-little-things-you-didnt-know-about-bob-ross
[2] http://heatonist.com/hot-ones-hot-sauce/

64

It was seriously funny. The host, Sean Evans, asks celebrity guest 10 questions, during which both Evans and the guest eat one chicken wing. Each wing is seasoned with progressively hotter hot sauce: the first is the mildest wing; the last is the hottest. Evans interviews the guest as the two make their way through the hot wings. If the person sitting at the table finishes the wings, then he or she gets 30 seconds to plug whatever he/she wants.

Most guests never make it to the 10th one.

As they go along, Evans describes each sauce, including one from their own company, always No. 5 on the list. The Hot Ones Hot Sauce, a mix of chipotle pepper, ghost pepper, habañero pepper, pineapple, and lime, was made for the show by Phoenix, Arizona-based Homeboy's Hot Sauce—and it's for sale.

Evan's interview style is casual, as one would imagine while eating hot wings, and the questions are excellent—not at all the run-of-the-mill interview stuff we're all used to seeing. When asked about preparation on a recent Reddit AMA, Evans said, "I usually spend at least 12 hours (sometimes a lot more) just watching every interview and reading everything I can find [about the guest]. We bring all our research together, then we kind of bring it all together and match the questions with the right wings so there's a good flow to the show.

"Our main goal with Hot Ones is for the guest to have fun and feel like they can be free and loose, so it's important to me for them to know that we went the extra mile to understand what they're all about, and ask about the shit that other people might leave on the cutting room floor."[3] We love that commitment to quality content. They want guests to feel special and put in the work to make it happen, rather than simply rely on the spectacle.

We basically lost a day to these videos, watching eight in a row and losing our minds laughing. Guests have included Michael Rapaport, Key and Peele, Ricky Gervais, Padma Lakshmi, Kevin Hart, and Dax Sheppard. Alison especially loves them because they've provided vegetarian and vegan options for past guests, while keeping the food hot of course. Evans is

---

[3] https://www.reddit.com/r/IAmA/comments/5x4bgy/hi_im_sean_evans_host_of_first_we_feasts_hot_ones/

an amazing interviewer and hot-sauce eater. Hilarity ensures, the conversation is engaging, and watching them react to the hot sauce is nothing short of magnificent. We subscribed to the channel, and looked for the sauce online. They didn't even need to give us a coupon, or ask for a like on Facebook.

Think about that for a minute. We are as jaded as can be, as you'd expect from two people who spend their lives online evaluating marketing practices and customer-service disasters.

And we subscribed, happily. Imagine subscribing to all the ads you see every day, the way we did for Hot Ones—ads for laundry detergent, or soft drinks, and even ads for other hot sauces!

Our lesson here is that content marketing isn't the key to success in our innovative branding world alone; you can't leave out all the factors that make it successful. These are videos you have to see, because of all the preparation and creativity that have gone into making them. They bring eyes to the brand. How often have you told someone they have to see a commercial? We'd bet our hot sauce this is the first time.

Lesson 24

A Lesson in Getting That Dream Job

A DAY DOESN'T GO BY that we aren't thankful for growing up before social media appeared. We made it through adolescence without a searchable database of embarrassing photos, without phones to distract us in school, without the horror of parents with Facebook accounts . . . We don't know how our kids do it.

Social-media education has been added to the parenting must-do list. Kids need to understand that the online world happens in public and that anything they share (or have shared about themselves) can follow them into the future: to college, job interviews, workplaces, and relationships. And it's not just kids who need this education. We are reminded daily that far too many people type and send without thought to consequences.

Personal branding matters.

On the flip side, the online world allows us to show our awesomeness with ease. We have no better example of this than Sumukh Mehta and his amazing résumé made for British GQ *Magazine*. The fact that we even know about someone's résumé sent to a magazine in another country we are in no way affiliated with is in itself a perfect example of disruptive technology. We considered creating a job just so that we could offer it to him. How's that for successfully getting the word out that you need a job?

Mr. Mehta's résumé to GQ[1] was a 20-page personal branding magazine, all about his accomplishments, experience, education, and why they should hire him, all done in the magazine's classic style. Needless to say, he got the internship without an interview and the résumé was shared around the world.

Photo credit: Sumukh Mehta

[1] http://mashable.com/2016/06/20/gq-magazine-resume/

The online world has given us countless digital tools to do cool digital things and ways to share our lives and loves with others. We have access to connections around the world and in our own neighborhoods. We checked out some of the many job search apps on the market today and were amazed by the options for personalization and depth of services, such as virtual career coaches to guide you on the way to your dream job. In the interval between writing this book, publishing it, and the time you take to read it, no doubt even more options will appear.

Our lesson here is that while Mr. Mehta chose to demonstrate his creativity (suitably so for the position he wanted) and others will jump into an app where they post videos and access career-planning tools, most of us will still get our jobs using one page, neatly spaced, with a cover letter and résumé. Don't miss out on the job you want because you're sidetracked trying to be someone you're not. If your goal is a creative job, be creative. If your would-be employer wants a traditional application, don't send them a video link alone and expect to wow them. Everyone is busy, so make it convenient for people to find you and hire you by focusing on the specific job and the roles and responsibilities it requires. A solid résumé is more valuable and effective than a bad video you made because that's what your new app told you to do. And remember that Facebook post you wrote last week about skipping your current job to day-drink with your friends: your would-be boss is going to see that too.

Lesson 25

The Value of Content-First Media

As an editor at Today's *Parent Magazine* and now at *Chatelaine*, Haley Overland has seen firsthand how digital innovations have affected the print-media industry. Back in 2010, the business was print focused. Ms. Overland was part of a tiny digital group who took print-focused content online, adjusting headlines for search engine optimization, adding sub-titles, and shortening content to make it more consumable on the go.

As digital media grew, there was a notion of integrating the teams. Editors would now have to know both print and digital and see stories all the way through from print to social media. While this gave the print department experience in digital, it also forced online writers and editors to work on print, something that for many seemed unnecessary. This type of integration couldn't work.

Today, *Chatelaine* is content driven—content first, digital first. The magazine recently announced that it would be moving from monthly to bi-monthly print editions, with sister magazine *Flare* moving to digital only. These are market-driven changes, as more and more readers choose to read content online. Ms. Overland also believes that it's value driven, since online content can include video and social media, options simply not available on newsstands.

The move to video has been one of the biggest innovations of digital. *Chatelaine* has a dedicated video team, creating video content and stopping thumbs. Content is driven by which articles most resonated with readers, something that can be easily measured and effectively used to draw more eyes to *Chatelaine*'s content.

Being content focused also allows *Chatelaine* to share content between magazines. Similar stories, if appropriate, can be put out to a variety of audiences. This allows them to focus on good content and then get the most out of it, rather than spreading themselves thin on quality to achieve quantity.

If Ms. Overland could share one lesson with brands it would be, "to see innovation as an opportunity. It allows us to reach more people who wouldn't otherwise see our magazine. We bring these eyes to important issues, women's issues. We are able to tell them our stories because we can go to where they are. Don't feel overwhelmed by social media. A lot of people in the industry who feel comfortable in print are nervous about making the transition. Just get started!"[1]

---

[1] Haley Overland, interview with authors.

Lesson 26

How to Go from One Star to Four

IN THE BOOK OF BUSINESS UNAWESOME, we wrote about how customers don't see silos. While you understand your business as a collection of departments, each with its own set of responsibilities and tasks, customers view your brand as one entity. When customers tweet a question or concern, they don't care if they've reached the social-media department or the intern you've placed flippantly to deal with "those millennials"; in their mind they've contacted the company and need to be treated that way. There is nothing more frustrating to our market than customers being told they've lined up in the wrong line, real or virtual. Make transitioning them to the right department an internal process, not an excuse not to handle whatever they're brought forward. You can't pass the branding buck; you need to empower employees—all employees—to access the answers your market demands.

Here is one story from a fan of the UnMarketing page about silos and branding. Jeremy Roberts wrote, "Being an Edmontonian, I used to love The Brick up until last year. We bought multiple items from them, furniture and appliances. The change came after we purchased a new washer and dryer with the promise of free installation. The 'installers' were the delivery guys, who didn't hook up the water connections properly. First load of wash flooded our basement and ruined our carpet. The Brick head office blamed the sales guy for promising free install as delivery guys aren't supposed to be doing that. The sales guy refused to admit he offered it at all. The store kept telling us to call head office. Head office told us to deal with the store. A year later, there's no resolution. I will never shop there again, and will never recommend them to anyone."[1]

Here we see how passing the blame for customer experience can ruin your brand. If your delivery service is bad, you need to hire a new delivery service, not shift blame onto the existing one when faced with customer complaints. Every point of contact between your company and your market is an opportunity to improve your brand perception.

When Monica B. ordered some furniture from Ashley HomeStore she left a happy customer. And a happy customer she remained—that is, until the furniture arrived at her home. It was delivered on the wrong day. It was the wrong furniture. And the wrong furniture, on the wrong day, was broken. The delivery crew were rude and left her with the wrong, broken furniture. As you can imagine, she was no longer a fan of Ashley HomeStore. She went onto Yelp and left the store a scathing review, a one-star rating (the lowest available), describing in detail all the delivery issues.

You might think this would be the end of the story, but Monica later went back and changed her review to a positive one, with a four-star rating—unheard of.

From Yelp in her own words (shown on the next page), here's why:

After my scathing Yelp review, I was immediately (and I mean immediately) contacted by the owners. Ben is courteous, professional, and kind. He followed up with everything he stated he was going to do very promptly. His apology felt sincere, and because of him I don't think I'd hesitate to shop at one of the Ashley stores he owns.

---

[1] https://www.facebook.com/UnMarketing/posts/10155288147715942

Monica B.
University of Texas,
Austin, TX
👥 10 friends
⭐ 10 reviews

⭐⭐⭐⭐⭐ 6/3/2014

To be fair (as I strive to be in any online review), I am updating my review. It is an average of the following:

Original In-Store Experience: 4-star
Salesperson Follow-Up/Post Purchase Experience: 1-star
After Yelp Review Experience: 5-star
Delivery Experience: 5-star
Total: 3.75 stars, rounded up to 4.

After my scathing Yelp review, I was immediately (and I mean immediately) contacted by the owner. Ben is courteous, professional, and kind. He followed up with everything he stated he was going to do very promptly. His apology felt sincere, and because of him I don't think I'd hesitate to shop at one of the Ashley stores he owns.

Ben gets it. This is how you need to handle silo mistakes in your company. Take responsibility, act promptly, and fix the problem. Ben didn't throw the delivery people under the bus; he took responsibility and came out looking even better after the screw-up than he did before. Our lesson here is to be more like Ben. Your customers don't see a set of departments, silos, or even franchises; they see your brand, and how you choose to act affects that brand.

You always have an opportunity to create a positive brand experience for your customers, and you always have the ability to move the needle. You just need to start by owning each and every customer's experience as your responsibility. No matter what your business card says, we are all responsible for branding. Rather than stewing over a negative review or shifting the blame to the review site itself, be like Ben. You'll find you end up with an even better review than you could have had without the screw-up.

Lesson 27

Quenching the Brand Thirst

GATORADE HAS THE KIND OF brand recognition we dream of. Who needs to pay the big bucks for a Super Bowl ad when your product gets dumped all over the winning team, right? That is, unless you sell anvils (social-media manager for Wile E. Coyote perhaps), or Big Ass Fans (http://www .bigassfans.com), or cars, I guess—because that would just be weird and messy. You know what we mean. Gatorade is synonymous with winning and sports—two pretty big branding ideas.

The creator of Gatorade,[1] Dr. Robert Cade, started back in 1965 at the University of Florida as an assistant coach, just looking to improve his football team's performance on the field. His researchers realized that the heat was affecting the players, who were becoming dehydrated during practices and games. Tests showed Dr. Cade that they were losing vital fluids and electrolytes, which weren't being replaced. When the first prototypes of a fluid-replacement drink tasted awful, his wife suggested adding lemon juice to the mix, and the product was born, named after the team—the Gators.

---

[1] http://fortune.com/2015/10/01/gatorade-turns-50/

When the drink worked, word began to spread and yadda, yadda, yadda on January 25, 1987, linebacker Harry Carson poured a bucket of the stuff on New York Giants head coach Bill Parcells after defeating the Denver Broncos during Super Bowl XXI, and the "Gatorade dunk" or "Gatorade shower" was born. Former endorsers of the brand include Michael Jordan and Mia Hamm. Even Peyton Manning (our favorite athlete turned commercial star) has lent his persona to the brand.

Obviously, the "yadda, yadda, yadda" portion of the story is important. There's the timing factor; at the time Gatorade was developed it was big science. The ability of physiologists at the school to figure out what was going on for the athletes on the field was a huge development, and there was no competition at the time in this space. As consumers, when we started being able to watch football games on TV, Gatorade was already a staple. There was no bidding for product placement at the games. It was clear; if we wanted to feel strong and healthy like football players, we should drink what they were drinking.

This is a great example of a brand that is difficult to learn from because of the breadth of its success. Unless your product or service has developed an entirely new space, it would be impossible for a growing brand today to do what Gatorade did and be successful. To us, what is more important than the brand's history are the lessons found in how it is managing social media today. Gatorade has a social-media mission control center inside its home office in Chicago. We're talking about a giant room that has six large monitors running custom applications from Radian6 and IBM, all keeping track of and analyzing conversations online about the brand, its competitors, and terms related to its market (such as "sporting events" and anything related to "fitness" or "nutrition"). It uses the data to engage and also to create relevant content.

For example, according to Gatorade's senior marketing director and consumer and shopper-engagement head, Carla Hassan, the control center is used in "the company's monitoring of its 'Gatorade has evolved' campaign. The commercials featured a song by rap artist David Banner, which, the mission-control team quickly realized, was being heavily discussed in social media. Within 24 hours, they had worked with Banner to put out a full-length version of the song and distribute it to Gatorade followers and fans on Twitter and Facebook, respectively."

Ms. Hassan has said that the goal of the mission-control project is to "'take the largest sports brand in the world and turn it into the largest participatory brand in the world.'"[2] Gatorade is actively listening to everything, taking that listening and turning it into action, such as enabling fans to interact with athletes and health experts via Ustream.

Now before you call a contractor, we aren't suggesting you turn your garage into a social-media control center. But you can take a lesson from Gatorade and allocate the time and resources you have available to listen, engage, and then take that information and use it to shape your business. If you're only reacting to negative feedback, you're missing the point. Listening and engagement isn't a campaign. It's not something to be done once a year or for a week (day or hour) right before you launch your new product.

For example, if you're the anvil salesperson we mentioned earlier, you'd be focusing on your brand name and on your competitors, but you'd also be using terms like "forging," "steel," and, of course, "Looney Tunes." Our Gatorade lesson is that the data you need to build customer loyalty is out there; you just have to be paying attention and willing to react. The beauty of content marketing is in positioning yourself as an expert, and listening lets you know where to stand.

---

[2] http://mashable.com/2010/06/15/gatorade-social-media-mission-control/

Lesson 28

Samsung Swansong

OH MY, WHERE TO START with this one. So many issues, so little time. We think for Samsung we'll just make a list.

1. The Samsung beautification app. Who among us hasn't edited a selfie to look a little less tired? We've all done it. There are lights you can attach to your phone, features inside Instagram and Snapchat and apps like FaceTune all dedicated to putting your best selfie forward. Think of it as online makeup. But when it came to light that Samsung phone cameras were automatically editing photos, people were less than impressed. Author and health coach Mel Wells shared on Instagram her frustration with Samsung when after buying a new phone, she went to take a selfie but was surprised to see the face looking back at her had been "heavily edited." The *Green Goddess Revolution* author, who is also an activist for positive body image, wrote "the default setting on the front camera is automatically on 'Beauty level 8,' which evidently means 'seriously airbrushed face.'" She went on to write, directed to the Samsung account, "this means everyone who gets a new Samsung phone and flicks the front camera on is automatically being told, 'Hi,

we're Samsung, and we think you look way better when we automatically airbrush your selfies for you, x 8!'. Thanks @samsungmobile for the vote of confidence, I think I'll keep my freckles and imperfections since this is how I look in 3D, and this is how all my friends see me in real life."[1]

2. The Samsung explodiness of things. After reports of exploding and overheating batteries, Samsung was forced to discontinue sales of its Galaxy Note 7 because people are leery about carrying explosives around in their pockets. Then we started seeing pictures of signs at airlines banning Samsung phones from flights, like one Scott took:

[1] http://www.cosmopolitan.com/uk/beauty-hair/news/a44232/samsung-beautify-mode/

Who needs their phones for travel really, right? It's only where we keep our contacts, calendar, hotel information, GPS so we don't get lost, dictionaries for help with translations, entertainment for the trip, and the highly important boarding passes!

3. Our son wanted a pair of wireless Samsung headphones for Chanukah, but they won't sync to iPhones, only to Samsung phones, which seem to be exploding. So we got him a Bose pair instead.

4. And then there's the whole Samsung washing-machine situation. Last year, Samsung recalled nearly 3 million washing machines after complaints about violent vibrations, "explosions," and one broken jaw.[2] The company offered the choice of an in-home repair, a rebate on a new machine, or a complete refund for recent purchases. After several months, many customers were reporting frustration with all of the options.

There's a lot to be learned about branding your product better. We can teach you about tools and tricks to spread the word and build community around your product or service. We can solve branding problems. But when your products anger customers, don't work, or explode, you don't have a branding problem; you have a business problem. Our Samsung lesson, other than making sure you have a well-funded research and development department that does stringent product testing before going to market, is that social media is only an amplification tool designed to make your voice louder. Start with a product you can be proud of before building your brand, because when your product is ugly, there's no brand filter that can help you.

---

[2] https://consumerist.com/2017/03/01/vanishing-rebate-checks-canceled-appointments-stories-of-samsungs-turbulent-washer-recall/

Lesson 29

Doctor Wanted: Must Not Have Facebook

SOCIAL MEDIA IS OFTEN A place we vent about negative experiences. Stories about long lines, disappointing food, and the daily grind must take up about 92% of all Internet traffic. Most of the complaints never reach outside our circle, and the vast majority aren't aimed at those actually causing the complaints.

When Sarah Rubio posted a message on a private Facebook group about a negative experience with her pediatrician, she was simply looking for some support from her community. She never could have predicted that the complaint would make its way to the doctor's office; as a result the doctor promptly dropped her and several other moms who'd commented on her post as patients. We guess not every individual in the group, made up of several thousand members in all, valued its "private" nature. Someone had taken screenshots of the post and comments and sent them along to the office.

Now legally, doctors are within their rights to drop patients as they see fit, but something being legal is not always the same as something being right or good for business. When you Google the doctor's office name, the whole thing comes up on the first page. The story made the news, which is where we heard about it[1]. When we looked into this doctor's office, we found many negative reviews and a derogatory two-star rating on Yelp[2] along with some pretty brutal comments. Perhaps rather than drop unsatisfied patients, this doctor should be taking some of this feedback to heart, and it seems Ms. Rubio was far from being the only one with complaints.

Our lesson here is twofold: from the business perspective, when you receive negative feedback make sure you take it to heart, especially if it's coming from a variety of sources as was the case here. If one angry customer says you need improvement that's one thing, but when the vast majority of your clients are complaining, it's time to take a look and make some changes. From the patient's perspective, we ask you to remember that nothing you post or share online is truly private; it is all a reflection of you and your values. Please don't be fooled by the intimate nature of a private group, chat, email, or even text message into thinking the things you type can't or won't become public.

---

[1] https://www.facebook.com/pages/Island-Coast-Pediatrics/114886818567459

[2] https://www.yelp.com/biz/island-coast-pediatrics-cape-coral?osq=Island+Coast+Pediatrics

Lesson 30

InSuencer Marketing

INSTAGRAM ALLOWS ANYONE TO BE fashion famous. Unlike fashion magazines where models, musicians, and actors show us what's hip (Do people still say "hip"? We probably should have checked this one with the kids), on Instagram anyone can become a fashion icon. Need an idea for how to wear your hair to a party? How about make-up tips and tutorials? Cool outfit suggestions with side-by-side photos? Instagram has it all. Without editorial gatekeepers, all it takes is the will, the time, and the right content to attract attention.

It didn't take long for fashion brands to recognize the digital shift. They jumped into the platform with both feet, with their own accounts and marketing campaigns geared to get their products into the hands of influencers. In the brave new world of digital, the rules took some time to develop. Influencers who were paid for their promotions, either monetarily or in free product, needed to let their followers know that these were commercials. This disclosure is mandatory and must be done in a way that is clear and obvious to their followers. The notice must be placed close to the content, not on a separate page on the website.

Disclosure has been a challenge for brands and influencers alike. For those who built a following on their honest opinions and sharing, maintaining their reach while earning money and free product has been a struggle. Influencers are still learning to walk the line between sponsored and non-sponsored content. For brands, disclosure was a roadblock to the kind of content marketing they hoped social media would provide. They wanted it to appear as though the Instagram stars really loved them, but paying for exposure came with rules. And as national retailer Lord & Taylor found out, the rules had teeth.

Lord & Taylor settled with the Federal Trade Commission over charges that they deceived consumers by paying for "native advertisements, including a seemingly objective article in the online publication *Nylon* and a *Nylon* Instagram post, without disclosing that the posts actually were paid promotions for the company's 2015 Design Lab clothing collection. As part of the Design Lab rollout, Lord & Taylor paid 50 online fashion influencers to post Instagram pictures of themselves wearing the same paisley dress from the new collection but failed to disclose they had given each influencer the dress, as well as thousands of dollars, in exchange for their endorsement."[1]

It takes hundreds of pictures and posts to build trust on Instagram and only one paid-for paisley dress to break it. The brand lesson here is *disclose, disclose, disclose*.

---

[1] https://www.ftc.gov/news-events/press-releases/2016/03/lord-taylor-settles-ftc-charges-it-deceived-consumers-through

Lesson 31

UnLove Shack

RADIO SHACK WAS A STAPLE of our childhood. Before giant tech super stores, before Amazon, Radio Shack was the place to find cutting-edge stuff—that cool VCR tape rewinder that looked like a car, remote-control anything, and oh so many cables. Like the car phone in a bag you could buy there, the relevance and success of the brand diminished over the years, and the company recently filed for bankruptcy.

We want to look back fondly at Radio Shack, but they haven't been making it easy for us.

On episode No. 170 of the *UnPodcast*, "The Coffee is Cold,"[1] we looked at some companies that blur the ethics of discount pricing by bumping up original costs, never actually selling items at said original cost, and then offering their customers exciting (fake) discount prices. Much to our disappointment, Radio Shack decided to take the ethical elevator down a few floors and promote sale prices that were actually higher than the original prices. That's right—higher.

---

[1] http://www.unmarketing.com/2017/04/19/170-the-coffee-is-cold/

Some Radio Shack employees reached out to Consumerist.com with news that the retailer had raised "original" or list prices on hundreds of items shortly before the Shack's March 8 bankruptcy filing, presumably to give the appearance that the subsequent "clearance" sale offered deeper discounts than if the base price had not changed. However, we can now see that some of the items on Radio Shack's website are now selling for *more* than they were only weeks before the chain went bankrupt.[2]

Now we know people love to feel like they're getting a deal, but there actually has to be a deal to get. Perhaps the company doesn't care much about branding anymore; it just wants to grab whatever it can to make it through its bankruptcy filing. Perhaps this was all a huge mistake, the result of using a computer system from the late 1980s to manage its inventory—we aren't sure. The branding lesson here is to remember that prices ought to be managed ethically; calling a price increase a sale is unethical and bad for business.

We guess the sale prices didn't work out too well, because Radio Shack recently closed hundreds of stores. However, they forgot one tiny thing—to take away the stores' fired employees' access to the stores' social-media accounts, which had pretty hilarious results. One such account, the Facebook page of former Radio Shack no. 4831 in Reynoldsburg, Ohio,[3] has become popular as a result of the particularly glorious postings that have appeared since the store closed. Just check out the page header:

[2] https://consumerist.com/2017/03/21/some-radioshack-items-were-actually-cheaper-before-they-went-on-clearance-sale/

[3] https://consumerist.com/2017/04/19/radioshack-stops-caring-brushes-off-profane-posts-by-rogue-closed-store/

Adios. We see what you did there.

It is a special kind of social-media irony to see just how creative and popular the page can be. It might have been useful for the company a few quarters ago.

Some of the posts have been a tiny bit angry, as you can see in what follows. But when you fire people, close their location, and continue to allow them to access a branded account, you're kind of asking for things like these:

Because of these things, Radio Shack was trending online. The store page has a 4½-star rating now, likely higher than it ever had while it was open, with customers posting reviews like this one:

> Went in to buy batteries. The salesman said: "Batteries? I'll show you battery!" and proceeded to beat me with an RC car. Not sure what happened next, but I woke up outside with my pants unbuttoned, and a new pack of AA batteries in my pocket. Definitely will miss this place. 5/5

The lesson here is that when you fire people, you should probably take away their social-media keys along with their parking passes and other stuff.

Or maybe it's that whoever is running this page was clearly undervalued for their creativity; who knows what they could have done for the company in the name of good branding? We'll never know. But either way, thank you, Radio Shack store no. 4831, you gave us and a whole lot of other people something to smile about.

Lesson 32

What's in a Name

IT'S ONE OF THE THINGS business owners sweat over: what to name their company and its products. We usually brush this kind of thing off at UnMarketing to focus on more important things in branding, like making your company great. No one buys an iPhone because Apple is the perfect name for a company. Aside from that, we get it. You want a name you love, something meaningful. Scott came up with the name UnMarketing because he thought it would look great on a book cover (little did he know). Two people who created UnMarketing, UnSelling, the *UnPodcast*, and now UnBranding shouldn't really be lecturing you about worrying what your stuff is called.

If you want some inspiration in why a brand name matters, look no further than the marijuana industry. It's a growing industry, and moving into legalization has companies second-guessing their product names. The question is: Would Atomic Haze by any other name still smell as sweet? Moving into legalization means that a change in reputation and perception is possible and that what the product is called sets the stage for all that. According to Bloomberg, "a pot company called 1906 (named for the year the government first went after marijuana) is moving from traditional weed names into more mainstream monikers for its cannabis-infused chocolates. For example, there's Go (energy booster), Pause (relaxing), Midnight (sleep aid), Present (for focus), and High Love (for getting busy)."[1]

That seems like a good business move to us. We aren't suggesting you focus all or even most of your energy on naming, but we do think you should consider market perceptions when you do. Chose something meaningful to you, something you're passionate about, something you can see in giant neon lights. Make sure you search for other companies that may be using that name or a similar one and consider its possible meanings. And don't be too hard on yourself if you make a few naming blunders along the way. When Mercedes-Benz first moved into the market in China, they marketed under the brand name Bensi, which means "rush to die." Ford sold the Pinto in Brazil, but it didn't get the kind of attention they were expecting, mostly because *pinto* there means "tiny male genitals."[2]

---

[1] https://consumerist.com/2017/01/26/marijuana-companies-trading-stoner-slang-for-mainstream-branding/

[2] https://www.inc.com/geoffrey-james/the-20-worst-brand-translations-of-all-time.html

Lesson 33

Loyalty Makeup

FOR CHANUKAH, TESSA WANTED MAKE-UP to play with at home. She loves make-up, as only the daughter of a woman who owns none and can't apply it to save her life could. And so, Alison made her first journey into the make-up giant Sephora. It was shiny and beautiful, totally overwhelming. A perfectly made-up woman handed her a basket and helped her navigate more colors and brushes than she'd ever imagined. At 41, Alison bought her first make-up—a collection for a 10-year-old.

We know from Instagram, friends, and family that Sephora is awesome. It's in our local mall, so proximity was key to the choice. The online search for make-up was just too vast, and since the store promised assistance and a variety of products, the choice was clear. Alison's personal experience with the store was good, and the gift successful—a happy branding story.

So when in March we saw this story about Sephora in *Teen Vogue*, we were thrilled. There's nothing better to us than seeing a brand we personally have loved doing good in the world. It makes us feel all warm and fuzzy inside.

The company just launched their Brave Beauty in the Face of Cancer class nationwide, a free, 90-minute workshop for both men and women undergoing cancer treatments. On one level, the class provides a forum for people to pick up tips on dealing with hair loss and skin sensitivities. The "class for confidence" allows customers to "discover techniques and products that address the visible effects of cancer treatments" with tailored skin-care tips, Color IQ skin-matching, and a step-by-step tutorial. But, more important, it's also a safe space that allows patients to come together and connect in an empowering environment.[1]

The branding lesson here is that giving back is important, especially when it goes hand in hand with great products and service, provided in a way that makes it easy for us to give you our money. Alison may not need to venture back into a Sephora any time soon, but when she does need makeup, the choice will be crystal clear.

gue.com/story/sephora-brave-beauty-in-the-face-of-cancer-free-class

Lesson 34

Skee-Ball Is Forever

CHUCK E. CHEESE IS LIKE Las Vegas for kids. We grew up with it; we have memories of birthday parties, the ball pit (which seemed so enormous at the time), and counting tickets before there were machines for that to trade for prizes our parents could have bought us for pennies. We've taken our kids; we sat eating pizza, wondering why they don't have branded earplugs. When we started doing research for *UnBranding*, Chuck E. Cheese was at the top of the list of companies we wanted to learn more about. Just how had the idea come about, and how had it survived through innovations in gaming, dining, and entertainment?

It turned out, there was one man responsible, and he'd done much more than give us an animatronic band and a Vegas gateway drug. The Chuck E. Cheese concept was developed by Atari co-founder Nolan Bushnell,[1] who brought games like Pong into the mainstream. He was responsible for our generation's love of video games—and possibly for our

---

[1] https://www.theatlantic.com/technology/archive/2013/07/chuck-e-cheeses-silicon-valley-startup-the-origins-of-the-best-pizza-chain-ever/277869/

obesity problem as well. He brought together two great loves—pizza and video games—and for that, we will always be grateful.

Bushnell explained, "It was my pet project. I started it inside Atari. My objective was to vertically integrate the market. We were selling coin-operated games at about $1,500 or $2,000 a pop. In their life, they'd make $15 to 20k. It didn't take rocket science to say I'm on the wrong side of the equation. I didn't want to compete with the people I was selling to, but the game operating business is all about securing locations. So the way to not compete with them was to secure my own locations. The original genesis was to create a big arcade with food as a support structure, almost as an ancillary service."[2] He saw an opportunity to secure locations by opening his own.

When he traveled to a trade show, he saw a mascot and chose it for the chain, thinking it was a coyote. That is, until his employees let him know it was actually a rat. We think everyone can agree that rats and food aren't exactly a winning combination, but somehow they made it work. After some brainstorming, they changed the name from the planned Coyote Pizza to Chuck E. Cheese and the chain was born.

Choosing pizza as the food staple was a choice made in the name of simplicity. As Bushnell explained, "I chose pizza because of the wait time and the build schedule: very few components and not too many ways to screw it up. If the dough is good, the cheese is good, and the sauce is good, the pizza is good. I didn't have any preconceived idea that I knew how to run a restaurant, but I knew simple was better."[3] When making choices for your business, remember these words. Simple is always better, and when you're looking to do something on a large scale, the fewer opportunities there are for mistakes, the less chance you have of making them.

One of the features of Chuck E. Cheese that has changed over the years is the entertainment. Back in our day, there was a separate room with a stage and an animatronic band of animals who would put on a show every

---

[2] https://www.theatlantic.com/technology/archive/2013/07/chuck-e-cheeses-silicon-valley-startup-the-origins-of-the-best-pizza-chain-ever/277869/.
[3] Ibid.

half hour or so. At the time, this was some cutting-edge stuff! The reason behind having the entertainment was ingenious: "The reason for doing the animals, believe it or not, was not for the kids. It was meant to be a head fake for the parents. Kids are really smart at knowing how to play their parents, and the kids knew that if they said, 'I want to go to Chuck E. Cheese and play the games,' the parents would just see themselves spending money. But if they said, 'I want to go see Chuck E. Cheese entertainment—and it's free,' they'd be good to go."

The most important lesson from Chuck E. Cheese is how it has maintained brand loyalty by focusing not only on what kids want but on what their parents want as well. You can't run a successful business for kids, without focusing on who's actually paying for everything, and of course who's got the car keys. The most successful kid's entertainment providers always remember the parents. We see this in Disney movies, where story lines and jokes are written to keep adults happy alongside children. Chuck E. Cheese has never forgotten this value and uses it in its marketing. Today, its menu includes salads, wraps, and other healthy options geared toward parents. It focuses on child safety, using a cool matching stamp system to link families and keep kids safe, and provides free Wi-Fi.

Sometimes we get lost in branding and forget who's paying the bills. We want to look cool or edgy, so we focus on what our competition is doing or on what we've always done. We jump around from platform to platform or focus only on the places and tools we love, while forgetting our market. Learn from Chuck E. Cheese and spend some time thinking about where your revenue comes from. Focus on customers' needs and wants, and let that be your guide through innovation. When Bushnell started out, he chose pizza for simplicity, but as times changed and parents wanted other options, Chuck E. Cheese provided them. When parents were no longer entertained by the animatronic band, they were given Wi-Fi. When concerns over child safety grew, technology was used to give families a greater sense of security.

Recently, Chuck E. Cheese rolled out Sensory Sensitive Sundays, held nationwide on the first Sunday of every month. For two hours before locations are open to the general public, staff dim the lights, turn off the music, and unplug the stage show to achieve "an environment more suitable for children who face sensory challenges." The initiative began when Amanda Moniz, an outreach coordinator for the Center for Autism and Related Disorders (CARD), approached the Chuck E. Cheese in Attleboro, Massachusetts, with a request: "Would you be willing to open two hours early for my nephew, who has autism?" The restaurant agreed and received enough positive press and reviews to reach head office, where Ami Anderson, the company's senior director for advertising and media advocated for it to become a regular offering in time for World Autism Awareness Day on April 2, 2017. To help make sure the events would be a success, CARD trained restaurant employees on how to work with autistic kids and spread the word. One of our favorite parts of the story is that Ms. Anderson said the monthly events have "added a new level of passion to our employees and our guests."[4] Articles called the events "innovative marketing" because of the positive results, but to us this is simply an example of Chuck E. Cheese continuing to focus on the needs of their customers, and choosing to be a human company.

Everything has changed about Chuck E. Cheese, and nothing is different. That's how to maintain a brand through disruptive times. That, and Skee-Ball. Because Skee-Ball is forever.

---

[4] http://www.adweek.com/brand-marketing/chuck-e-cheeses-lowers-the-lights-and-noise-once-a-month-for-kids-with-autism/

Lesson 35

You Can't Please Everyone

IT'S HARD, IF NOT IMPOSSIBLE, to please everyone. In marketing and branding, aiming to please as many people as possible can be a misstep because to do so, you usually need to be as muted and middle-ground as possible.

When we first saw the Toronto Transit Commission (TTC) campaign created in partnership with some other popular Toronto brands such as the Toronto Football Club and the Raptors, we loved it. Combining the city's public transport system with a local tourist attraction just made sense. The campaign was well received until the partnership with the Toronto Ballet.

The TTC and the Toronto Ballet are two iconic brands in the city; the images were beautifully done, and the "We Move You" tagline was brilliant for both brands. An example of one of the images is on page 98.

When we started reading about the negative feedback the campaign was receiving we were surprised—what were we missing? The ballet images were striking a chord the others had not—a very negative one. A group campaigning to have discrimination based on size and appearance made illegal in the province of Ontario had targeted the ads. Jill Andrew, co-founder of the Body Confidence Canada Awards, told the press that "the images send the wrong messages about what healthy, confident humans should look like."[1]

The past partnerships, also with professional athletes, had featured talented, athletic bodies, but for some reason these had avoided the conflict. The TTC maintained that the campaign was meant to highlight and "cross-promote the various elements that go into making Toronto a vibrant and thriving city," and did not remove the ads.

This goes to show that you can't possibly please everyone with your brand. From our perspective, the images were beautiful representations of the elite athletes our city was proud of. To someone who had experienced discrimination based on body shape and size, the images were upsetting and damaging to other riders on the TTC.

---

[1] https://www.thestar.com/news/gta/2016/10/27/ttc-ballet-campaign-gets-unflattering-review.html

The lesson for your brand is to make sure you are using images that represent your customers and your would-be market. If you're concerned about whether you're making the right choices, reach out to experts for feedback. Remember that how you see things may not be how your market will see them. In the end, strong messages and images make good marketing, but when you use them, you're bound to polarize. There will always be some who are offended by your work. When you make polarizing choices, make sure you are ready to stand behind your decisions.

Lesson 36

This Oatmeal Is Just Right

IF WE WERE AT ALL artistically inclined, we might try to draw this chapter rather than write it. But, we aren't, not even a tiny little bit. Thankfully, we don't need to be good at something (or even marginally passable at something) to love it. And oh how we love The Oatmeal; let us count the ways.

1. Launched in 2009 by artist Matthew Inman with three comics, the site had 5 million visits in its first month, and not one of the comics was about a Kardashian. Scott salivates over numbers like these, and that was just in the first month!
2. Exploding Kittens[1] —the game. We bought it, we love it, and we want more games.
3. The Oatmeal books—5 Very Good Reasons to Punch a Dolphin in the Mouth (and Other Useful Guides); How to Tell if Your Cat Is Plotting to Kill You; My Dog: The Paradox: A Lovable Discourse about Man's Best

---

[1] http://www.explodingkittens.com

Friend; and *Why Grizzly Bears Should Wear Underpants*. For the titles alone, we salute him. For the brilliant content, we adore him.

4. His cartoon about running, *The Terrible and Wonderful Reasons Why I Run Long Distances*[2] is Alison's favorite content on the subject, ever.

5. Inman won the Comic-Con Humanitarian Award in 2016.[3] The humanitarian award was created to honor people in comics and the popular arts who have worked to help others. We often think super-talented people don't also get to be kind, and that just doesn't seem fair. But Inman is truly both.

6. He creates content about things he's passionate about, not about things he's paid for. There are a lot of comics and mentions on The Oatmeal about Sriracha Hot Sauce—so many in fact that your marketing mind may think Sriracha sponsors the content, but it doesn't. He writes comics about Sriracha because he loves Sriracha.

7. He doesn't use search engine optimization (SEO) to drive content. "A lot of people ask, 'How do you do it?' I just make things that people like. SEO has no bearing on the Oatmeal,"[4] replies Matthew Inman, our hero.

8. He built his audience through social media. "Building and hanging on to an audience is the biggest role of social media. Then every time I make a comic, I can broadcast it out to them. That's been really helpful. I have this audience waiting for me. It's been awesome. You need to be funny and continually make them laugh. But when I started, I also had this [casually inviting] tone: 'Hey, guys, I just made a new comic—check it out!"[5] This is from Matthew Inman, our hero—again.

9. He makes money, in a way that he's proud of. "I did the donation thing, and I thought I would get a couple of dollars a day, but I

---

[2] http://theoatmeal.com/comics/running

[3] https://www.comic-con.org/awards/bob-clampett-humanitarian-award

[4] https://www.washingtonpost.com/blogs/comic-riffs/post/the-riffs-interview-12-secrets-of-insanely-viral-oatmeal-creator-matthew-inman/2011/03/11/ABM8JZR_blog.html?utm_term=.950ab2cf96fd.

[5] Ibid.

was getting a lot of traffic and it ended up being much more than that. I actually felt guilty, and I thought I should be giving them something in return, and that is when I decided to start selling merchandise—posters and stuff."[6] This is what Matthew Inman said, and you know who he is.

10. He fights against content theft—in the best possible way. In 2011, he called out user-generated site FunnyJunk[7] for reposting his comic strips without permission. The site took down some, but not all, of the content and about a year later sued Inman for defamation of character for $20,000. Rather than let it go, Inman shared the letter with his following in a truly fantastic blog post. He began a campaign to raise the money, not to pay FunnyJunk but for the National Wildlife Federation and the American Cancer Society. He ended up raising more than $220,000, and the lawsuit was eventually dropped.

11. And then there's his love for Nikola Tesla. Inman created an incredible cartoon called *Why Nikola Tesla Was the Greatest Geek Who Ever Lived*,[8] something we totally agree with by the way. In true Oatmeal style, it described all Tesla's accomplishments and how he'd been given very little credit. He didn't stop there; Inman created an Indiegogo campaign to buy back Tesla's old laboratory and turn it into a museum. The campaign ended up raising over $1.3 million and helped a nonprofit to buy back the land and to begin working on cleaning it up and hopefully one day building a museum to recognize Tesla's great works.[9]

Clearly, there is a lot to be learned from Matthew Inman and The Oatmeal. These lessons transcend the creative sphere and can be applied to all forms of business interactions. Still, we want to leave you with one lesson in particular: Matthew Inman says no. As he told the *Washington Post*:

"I got an offer from a deodorant company to write something for their advertising," Inman said, noting that he turned down the product

---

[6] http://chicagoist.com/2011/03/16/wild_oats_an_interview_with_matthew.php.

[7] http://theoatmeal.com/blog/funnyjunk

[8] http://theoatmeal.com/comics/tesla

[9] http://theoatmeal.com/blog/tesla_museum_saved

commission flat. "It's pretty much got to be a truly exceptional client. If it were Comedy Central, I'm all over that. Maybe if it [involves] an actor or actress I like. But Diet Coke, that's not gonna happen.[10]"

Saying no leaves space for opportunities, the kind of opportunities we really want. If you say yes to everything that comes along, you leave yourself very little room for integrity and for truly cultivating your own brand voice and audience. We know it's hard to risk turning things down, especially when they offer a financial benefit, but if you want to truly grow an innovation-proof business, you need to define your brand clearly with consistency and integrity.

---

[10] https://www.washingtonpost.com/blogs/comic-riffs/post/the-riffs-interview-12-secrets-of-insanely-viral-oatmeal-creator-matthew-inman/2011/03/11/ABM8JZR_blog.html

The Pooptastrophe

IF YOU AREN'T FAMILIAR WITH the Roomba, it's an "autonomous robotic vacuum cleaner," meaning you turn it on and it takes itself around your home or office cleaning up the floor. When it bumps into things, it changes direction without any additional work from you. So basically, the future is here, and we, for two, welcome our new Roomba overlords.

This year, we read the most incredible branding story about Roomba and one of their distributors, Hammacher Schlemmer, that we could imagine. It's everything we love about the Internet—funny, honest, and true to life—and we couldn't possibly write it better than the author himself, Jesse Newton. So with Jesse's permission, here in his own words is his Roomba story as it appeared on Facebook. We suggest you sit down.

So, last week, something pretty tragic happened in our household. It's taken me until now to wrap my head around it and find the words to describe the horror. It started off simple enough—something that's probably happened to most of you.

Sometime between midnight and 1:30am, our puppy Evie pooped on our rug in the living room. This is the only time she's done this, so

104

it's probably just because we forgot to let her out before we went to bed that night. Now, if you have a detective's mind, you may be wondering how we know the poop occurred between midnight and 1:30am. We were asleep, so how do I know that time frame?

Why, friends, that's because our Roomba runs at 1:30am every night, while we sleep. And it found the poop. And so begins the Pooptastrophe. The poohpocalypse. The pooppening.

If you have a Roomba, please rid yourself of all distractions and absorb everything I'm about to tell you.

Do not, under any circumstances, let your Roomba run over dog poop. If the unthinkable does happen, and your Roomba runs over dog poop, stop it immediately and do not let it continue the cleaning cycle. Because if that happens, it will spread the dog poop over every conceivable surface within its reach, resulting in a home that closely resembles a Jackson Pollock poop painting.

It will be on your floorboards. It will be on your furniture legs. It will be on your carpets. It will be on your rugs. It will be on your kids' toy boxes. If it's near the floor, it will have poop on it. Those awesome wheels, which have a checkered surface for better traction, left 25-foot poop trails all over the house. Our lovable Roomba, who gets a careful cleaning every night, looked like it had been mudding. Yes, mudding—like what you do with a Jeep on a pipeline road. But in poop.

Then, when your four-year-old gets up at 3am to crawl into your bed, you'll wonder why he smells like dog poop. And you'll walk into the living room. And you'll wonder why the floor feels slightly gritty. And you'll see a brown-encrusted, vaguely Roomba-shaped thing sitting in the middle of the floor with a glowing green light, like everything's okay. Like it's proud of itself. You were still half-asleep until this point, but now you wake up pretty damn quickly.

And then the horror. Oh the horror.

So, first you clean the child. You scrub the poop off his feet and put him back in bed. But you don't bother cleaning your own feet, because you know what's coming. It's inevitable, and it's coming at you like a freight train. Some folks would shrug their shoulders and get back in bed to deal with it in the morning. But you're not one of those people—you can't go to sleep with that war zone of poop in the living room.

So you clean the Roomba. You toss it in the bathtub to let it soak. You pull it apart, piece-by-piece, wondering at what point you became an adult and assumed responsibility for 3:30 am-Roomba-disassembly-poop-cleanups. By this point, the poop isn't just on your hands—it's smeared up to your elbows. You already heard the Roomba make that "whirlllllllllllllllll-boop-hisssssssss" noise that sounds like electronics dying, and you realize you forgot to pull the battery before getting it wet. More on that later.

Oh, and you're not just using profanity—you're inventing new types of profanity. You're saying things that would make Satan shudder in revulsion. You hope your kid stayed in bed, because if he hears you talking like this, there's no way he's not ending up in prison.

Then you get out the carpet shampooer. When you push it up to the rug—the rug that started it all—the shampooer just laughs at you. Because that rug is going in the trash, folks. But you shampoo it anyway, because your wife loved that damn rug, and you know she'll ask if you tried to clean it first.

Then you get out the paper towel rolls, idly wondering if you should invest in paper towel stock, and you blow through three or four rolls wiping up poop. Then you get the spray bottle with bleach water and hose down the floor boards to let them soak, because the poop has already dried. Then out comes the steam mop, and you take care of those 25-ft poop trails.

And then, because it's 6am, you go to bed. Let's finish this tomorrow, right?

The next day, you finish taking the Roomba apart, scraping out all the tiny flecks of poop, and after watching a few Youtube instructional videos, you remove the motherboard to wash it with a toothbrush. Then you bake it in the oven to dry. You put it all back together, and of course it doesn't work. Because you heard the "whirlllllllllllllllll-boop-hisssssssss" noise when it died its poopy death in the bathtub. But you hoped that maybe the Roomba gods would have mercy on you.

But there's a light at the end of the tunnel. After spending a week researching how to fix this damn $400 Roomba without spending $400 again—including refurb units, new motherboards, and new batteries—you finally decide to call the place where you bought it. That place called Hammacher Schlemmer. They have a funny name, but they have an awesome warranty. They claim it's for life, and it's for any reason.

So I called them and told the truth. My Roomba found dog poop and almost precipitated World War III.

And you know what they did? They offered to replace it. Yes, folks. They are replacing the Roomba that ran over dog poop and then died a poopy, watery death in the bathtub—by no fault of their own, of course.

So, mad props to Hammacher Schlemmer. If you're buying anything expensive, and they sell it, I recommend buying it from them. And remember—don't let your Roomba run over dog poop.[1]

We'll give you a few minutes to recover.

Hammacher Schlemmer has been in business for 169 years. It's a high-end catalog company known to offer cool and innovative products. In their own words, "from the beginning, our standards demanded quality, functionality and exemplary service. Some things should never change."[2]

We could not agree more. They provide pre-paid return slips with every order and even have a nonprofit, consumer-advocacy group that vets products to ensure they are in line with the levels of quality their customers have come to expect.

This is how you thrive through disruptive times. Not by putting all your focus on the next big marketing technology, but by providing quality products and service for your customers. Then when a brilliant writer like Jesse comes along, he does all that social media stuff for you. Don't be innovative for innovation's sake. Take care of your customers like Hammacher Schlemmer, and they will take care of your good name.

---

[1] https://www.facebook.com/jesse.newton.37/posts/776177951574
[2] http://www.hammacher.com/

Lesson 38

Scott Spratten, Kitten Killer

BACK IN 2013, WE RELEASED a picture book called *QR Codes Kill Kittens: How to Alienate Customers, Dishearten Employees, and Drive Your Business into the Ground*. The book was probably a little too much fun for us to make; it was a collection of pictures from businesses making generally horrible branding decisions, all in the name of looking cutting edge. The QR code was our poster child for using innovation for the sake of using it rather than because it made any actual business sense.

We knew the book would make people laugh (we couldn't stop laughing when we wrote it). We hoped the book would make people think and reconsider their "cool" marketing tactics. We were prepared for the dozens of notes and emails showing us their good QR codes (not shockingly, almost entirely from people who sold the tech or made money recommending it).

However, there was one unexpected consequence to the book: all the stuffed kittens we ended up sending out to concerned children. Here's one story from Brett and her mom that we shared on the *UnPodcast*.

I've been listening to the podcast since about Episode 6. My daughter, now five, has been listening with me this whole time. The other day in the car she says, "Mama, do you know Scott Spratten and Alison Kramer?"

"You mean from UnMarketing?"

"Yeah, the podcast people. You know, they have a friend named Emma. Like Miss Emma?

(Miss Emma is her gymnastics coach. All Emmas are Miss Emmas to her.)

"Okay yeah, I don't know them. They do the podcast. Why?"

"Can you tell me why they kill kittens and moron customers? They shouldn't do that."

(She laughs and tries to compose herself.)

"Oh honey, the saying 'kills kittens' is a way of saying something is no good. Something is so bad that it even kills cute little kittens. So if you think something is just rotten, you say it kills kittens."

"So no one kills kittens and eats their bones?"

"No."

"Do they kill customer morons?"

"No. That's a separate idea from the kittens. They say that customer service is an oxymoron. That means that businesses don't take good care of their customers."

"Okay good, so no one cooks up their customers' bones either?"

"No, Scott and Alison don't kill kittens or customers."

"I'm glad, Mama. I worried they did."[1]

We sent Brett a stuffed kitten and assured her we love kittens. What else could we do?

The lesson here for you is that you can't always predict who's listening, and you'd better have some budget put aside for personal brand repairs. We aren't sure who this Scott Spratten is, but we wouldn't hire someone who kills kittens and moron customers and cooks their bones. Would you?

---

[1] http://www.unmarketing.com/2016/07/20/132-no-brett-we-dont-kill-kittens/

Lesson 39

The Emperor Has No Juice

AT OUR HOUSE, JUICE IS a treat, like pop or ice cream. If you asked our kids, I'm sure they'd list it in the top-10 reasons why their friends are luckier than they are–right beside "my friend's mom lets her stay up until 10" and "but Mike down the street got his phone for his fifth birthday." Ah, the injustice. As far as Alison is concerned, you may as well just skip the liquid middleman and eat a whole heap of sugar. So when we read this story, you can imagine the smug look of righteousness on her face—it was glorious.

The Center for Science in the Public Interest, a consumer advocacy group, filed a lawsuit against PepsiCo for misleading marketing of its Naked Juice beverages. The misleading part was the bit where PepsiCo claimed its juice products were healthier than they really are. "Its Pomegranate Blueberry juice, for example, accurately advertises that it is a no-sugar-*added* beverage, but even still a single 15.2-ounce container (the smallest option) contains 61 grams of sugar, about 50% more sugar than a 12-ounce can of Pepsi."[1]

---

[1] http://www.businessinsider.com/pepsico-sued-for-naked-juice-marketing-2016-10

Now if PepsiCo had sold the drink as a sweeter, pulpier Pepsi, there wouldn't be a problem. The issue isn't about how healthy the juices actually are. The issue is with the company's marketing them as being healthy—a complete lie. The drinks are expensive, sold as such because of the healthful claims—using terms like "healthy" and "no-sugar added" and "all natural."

Ethical practices in the branding of food products are critical. We put a lot of trust in labeling when making decisions on what to eat and what to feed our families. So, when there are more pictures of strawberries on the Fruit Roll-Up box than inside the Fruit Roll-Up itself, we have a problem. General Mills agreed to improve the labeling of their "Strawberry Naturally Flavored Fruit Roll-Ups" after a lawsuit from a California woman and the nonprofit nutrition watchdog group the Center for Science in the Public Interest. It turned out that the roll-ups contained absolutely no strawberries at all "but are made with pears from concentrate, corn syrup, dried corn syrup, sugar, partially hydrogenated cottonseed oil, and 2 percent or less various natural and artificial ingredients."[2]

The labeling improvements mean that new labels will not include any images of strawberries.

While the lawsuit and changes made us feel a bit better about this particular product, it shows just how careful we all need to be about what's in our food. We need to be reading food labels and teaching our kids to do the same. We also need to be cautions of marketing claims used in advertising products as "natural, healthy, or made with real. . . ." as these can mean many different things.

The branding lesson here is to make sure your branding is in line with your actual product. We know it can be challenging to get attention and we all want to present as flashy and perfect, but false advertising only ends up making our real product look twice as bad. If you say you use real strawberries or are low in sugar, don't wait for a court case and a ton of negative attention to change up your marketing—just do better. Packaging is the cover we all use to judge the contents; don't let yours be real-life click bait.

---

[2] https://cspinet.org/news/general-mills-improve-strawberry-fruit-roll-ups-labeling-20121221

Lesson 40

The Kind of Branding Soulmate You Don't Want to Be

WE LOVE TOURISM CAMPAIGNS AND have been lucky to be invited to travel conferences around the world. Because we also love to travel, Scott's not only the keynote speaker at the event, he's also a customer, eager to check out new places and all the events and experiences they have to offer. We travel for business, alone for fun and also with our children, so we're interested in every option a location has to offer. We even started a travel podcast about Las Vegas called *The Vegas30*. It's for people over 30 who love Vegas, because it's a very different place in your 30s than it was in your 20s—you're too old to stand in line, too young to retire to bingo, so the Vegas30 is for you. Of course these days we need to change it to the Vegas40, but that's beside the point.

As much as we love travel, especially to Las Vegas, we hate theft. So when we read about Salt Lake City's campaign being brutally copied, we couldn't let it go. It seemed South Bend (Indiana) had mimicked Salt Lake's campaign—everything from the colors and fonts to the copy, as you can see in the following illustration.

The creative director responsible for the original campaign, Chip Haskell, shared a letter he sent to the South Bend agency:

All I can say is "Wow." As in, "Wow!" The color palette, the fonts, the headlines, the copy, the photos—they're all so cool and really work together! Now I hate to use the word "brilliant" unless I'm writing copy for a dentist who's selling some sort of whitening gel for people's teeth, so I won't use that word. Instead, I'll use the word "unbelievable"—as in, it's really unbelievable how fresh and awesome your campaign is.

Later in the letter, Haskell added:

What's important here is that Love and Explore Media have finally found one another and we didn't even have to use eHarmony or Tinder or that seedy section of Craigslist. Nope, we found each other naturally. And as far as I can tell, we're like marketing, video-producing soulmates of some sort.

Instead of wasting our efforts thinking up ideas independent of one another, we could maybe just use one another's ideas. . . . Of course, some people might have a real problem with this—even going so far as call it unethical or plagiaristic (if that's even a word)—but I choose to think of it as just being more efficient.[1]

The executive director of the creative team for South Bend admitted to being influenced by the Salt Lake campaign and wanting to do something similar. We do believe he was successful at that! The copycat video was eventually taken off-line, and apologies for the offense were given. The whole controversy touched on a subject we see every day and that we've had to manage ourselves. When you put content online and people are influenced by it, where is the line between being influenced and copying and stealing?

The line is in the credit—just how much credit is given and how obvious it is to people reading or watching that the idea/framework/ design isn't yours. If you're attempting in any way to hide where your influence came from, that's theft. So when you're reading this book and come upon a quote that inspires you, such as "You're not the jackass whisperer," or "If you believe business is built on relationships, make building them your business," or "Scott and Alison are literary geniuses," and you want to share those, please do; just remember to give credit within the content. Not in the comments, not in a line at the bottom of the scroll and not in a separate disclosure page but right wherever the content is being shared.

Our brand lesson here is that theft is bad for your (tourism) business. Stealing content makes you look bad, it negates the hard work of people you clearly admire; in the end, when it eventually happens to you, you'll have little defense. Share great work with credit—obvious credit.

And remember, when it comes to tourism it doesn't really matter how great your location is, how beautiful your design is, or how strong your campaign is, you'll never beat Okotoks.

---

[1] http://www.adweek.com/brand-marketing/south-bend-apologizes-lifting-salt-lakes-tourism-campaign-almost-wholesale-171695/

Lesson 41

Keeping the News en Vogue

ALISON LOVED TEEN MAGAZINES WHEN she was a kid for the clothes and the TV show gossip. At 11, the first thing she ever hung on her wall was a picture of Ralph Macchio, neatly cut from a coveted issue of *Teen Beat*. The idea that a magazine would actually be speaking to her and her interests was wonderful. When Tessa started reading, *National Geographic for Kids* was her favorite, as it had always been with her older brothers, although these days they're more interested in ESPN and the Uline catalog. As Tess has grown older, she's become more and more drawn to the teen fashion magazines, which left us trying to decide what would be appropriate for a 10-year-old who loves animals and justice and also fashion.

Teen Vogue caught our attention during the 2016 U.S. presidential election campaigns because it had some of the most interesting, well-researched, and thoughtful coverage around. We weren't the only ones who noticed, and the shock over a teen fashion magazine doing what so many media outlets had failed at was everywhere. The question is:

Why shouldn't *Teen Vogue* cover the election so well? The true shock should have been that so many other outlets were not.

In December 2016, *Teen Vogue* published an opinion piece by Lauren Duca called "Donald Trump Is Gaslighting America."[1] She compared the ways in which "the president-elect talks about his record to the ways abusive spouses psychologically manipulate their partners," and it struck a chord with readers on social media, earning 30,000 retweets and being shared by the likes of veteran TV journalist Dan Rather. While some of the shares were positive and respectful, many did so with a condescending tone toward the magazine, shocked that a teen magazine would publish something so thoughtful and well written. Clearly these individuals weren't familiar with *Teen Vogue* or with the history of women's magazines and their online community for providing strong political writing.

In 2016, *Teen Vogue* moved more and more into this arena. It didn't leave its popular culture focus behind; rather, it added a political viewpoint, something it felt its readers wanted. "In May, 29-year-old Elaine Welteroth took over as editor from Amy Astley, who helped found the magazine in 2003. Welteroth, the digital editorial director Phillip Picardi, and the creative director Marie Suter have moved the magazine more aggressively into covering politics, feminism, identity, and activism. Together, the three have shepherded a range of timely news stories, including an interview exploring what it's like to be a Muslim woman facing a Trump presidency, a list of reasons why Mike Pence's record on women's rights and LGBTQ rights should trouble readers, and a video in which two Native American teenagers from the Standing Rock Sioux tribe discuss the Dakota Access Pipeline protests."[2]

These are stories all media outlets should care about. *Teen Vogue* makes us feel hopeful for the future. Women's issues are human issues, and they shouldn't be segregated and devalued. This is especially critical for young women, who can create positive change in the world around them. These are the kinds of stories we want all our teenagers to be reading.

---

[1] http://www.teenvogue.com/story/donald-trump-is-gaslighting-america

[2] https://www.theatlantic.com/entertainment/archive/2016/12/teen-vogue-politics/510374/

"*Teen Vogue*'s September issue featured a personal essay by the presidential candidate Hillary Clinton, a conversation between the actor Amandla Stenberg and the feminist Gloria Steinem, and an interview with the U.S. attorney general, Loretta Lynch, conducted by the *Black-ish* star Yara Shahidi. The issue also introduced "21 Under 21,"[3] the magazine's "official guide to the girls and femmes changing the world." The list of young activists, artists, and advocates featured few household names but presented a notable majority of young people of color."[4]

As magazines struggle and lay blame for their struggle at the feet of the digital revolution, here is a magazine writing about what people need to hear and writing it well. Teenagers today have access to incredible amounts of information, and curators are vital. We all can learn from *Teen Vogue* about how to create thoughtful, intelligent content as well as how to have it reach the eyes and ears of its audience.

---

[3] http://www.teenvogue.com/story/21-under-21
[4] https://www.theatlantic.com/entertainment/archive/2016/12/teen-vogue-politics/510374/

Lesson 42

Send Loyalty
Sky High

I KNOW THIS WILL PROBABLY surprise all of you, but we actually do love a good brand story. Sure the trainwrecks are fun, but at the core of our seemingly bitter hearts, we love when customers are treated well and companies thrive. The bar isn't even set that high! Most branding and customer service is so terrible that a company only has to be mediocre to catch our eye. Put that on an inspirational poster, with a picture of an eagle flying into a mountain.

Anyway, that's why it's always nice to have a positive story, especially an airline story like this one. Qantas Airways announced recently that it would let "eligible frequent flyers keep their status for up to 18 months, even if they are not earning the number of status credits usually required to retain that tier. These members will also continue to enjoy their existing tier benefits, which may include lounge access, bonus points offers and preferred seating options."

This means loyal business customers who take time away from work for parental leave and other life changes that take away from their frequent trips won't lose their status or the points they've earned. Along with this announcement, they also launched another initiative parents will appreciate; it increased "its family transfer points limit and removed the restriction on the number of transfers. Members can now make an unlimited number of transfers to eligible family members up to 600,000 Qantas Points each year, compared to 400,000 previously."[1]

We love everything about this. As more and more loyalty programs (especially those in the travel industry) are tightening their belts, it's nice to see a company rewarding loyalty in a way that respects the choices of their customers. Our lesson from Qantas is to do just that—if you've worked hard to create a brand customers are loyal to, don't just let them go the minute they stop coming by. Loyalty is the most important defense against disruptive change, and it can be tremendously difficult to acquire. Remember you love these customers. They are your brand's ambassadors and defenders.

---

[1] http://www.nzherald.co.nz/business/news/article.cfm

Lesson 43

The Cheesy
ROI of Tattoos

A TATTOO AND A GREAT grilled-cheese sandwich are forever—and we love them both.

Scott has a bunch of tattoos. One on his forearm shows the word "unlearn," representing his belief that prejudice is taught and must be unlearned to make the world a better place. An audience member at a keynote once thought it said "unicorn," which was concerning for a number of reasons. So, for anyone reading who one day finds themselves in Scott's audience, if he wanted a unicorn on his arm, it would be a picture of a majestic unicorn, not the word "unicorn." Unlearn that.

Between us we have tattoos of a dragon, a lion, flowers, names (including each other's), flags, and medals, but not one of food. Not that there's anything wrong with food tattoos—Scott considers getting a BBQ tattoo every time we go to Nashville.

When we heard about Melt Bar and Grilled, a restaurant in Cleveland, Ohio, and their Melt Tattoo Family, we had a few questions. Just what did customers get for joining the tattoo family? What exactly did they have to get tattooed with to qualify? And just how good were these tattoo-worthy sandwiches? We needed to know.

According to the restaurant:

> A true testament to Melt's success is known as the "Melt Tattoo Family." What started as a half-joke promotion offering 25% off for life to anyone who would have the Melt logo tattooed on them exploded into what can only be described as a phenomenon in the restaurant industry. The Tattoo Family now boasts over 700 card-carrying members, each of them an ambassador for the little Cleveland restaurant that could, and did, capture a piece of their hearts.[1]

The restaurant's website even has a gallery of every tattoo and offers suggestions for tattoo shops. There's also a Big Cheese Club for those who prefer collecting points to collecting ink as well as the monster grilled-cheese challenge for those who choose to collect five pounds of food in their belly. If you finish it all you get a Melt T-shirt or Melt pint glass and a $10 gift card, and you are immortalized on the online Melt Challenge Hall of Fame. It's amazing the things people will do for a discount.

If you have a product people love enough to have it tattooed on their body, we think that's awesome and we definitely think we could all learn a brand lesson from Melt—be creative! Melt is giving their fans a bunch of ways to share their love of the restaurant, and in return it's creating community along with on-brand fun. Even without plans to get a Melt tattoo, eat the five-pound sandwich, or collect points, the restaurant just feels like a good place to hang out in while eating quality food. That's what branding is all about.

---

[1] https://www.facebook.com/meltbarandgrilled/videos/10153945547425728/

Lesson 44

Loyalty That Will Never Lego

LEGO IS A BRAND WE admire and is a fan favorite in our house. We grew up playing with the pieces, we love the sets and the collaborations with other great brands, and we even love the movies and video games.

This story caught our eye and made us even bigger fans than we already were. Luka, age 7, took his Ninjago Ultrasonic Raider set to the grocery store. This was the set he'd bought with all his Christmas money, the set his dad warned him not to bring to the store because it could get lost. Luka didn't heed the wise words; he took the set with him and lost one of the figures.

As a parent what do you do? You can't just replace the figure, which would usually require you to buy a whole new set. You warned Luka, and he decided not to listen, learning his lesson the hard way. You also love your child and know how sad he is, so you're sad too, because after he goes to bed, what are you going to play with now?

Luka's dad decided to help him write an email to Lego Customer Service explaining what happened to see if they could get a replacement. Here is Lego's reply:

Thanks for sending us an email!

We are very sorry to hear about you losing your Jay minifigure, but it sounds like your dad might have been right about leaving it at home. It sounds like you are very sad about it too.

Normally we would ask that you pay for a new one if you lose one of your minifigures and need to have it replaced. My bosses told me I could not send you one out for free because you lost it, but I decided that I would put a call into Sensei Wu to see if he could help me.

Luka, I told Sensei Wu that losing your Jay minifigure was purely an accident and that you would never ever ever let it happen ever again. He told me to tell you, "Luka, your father seems like a very wise man. You must always protect your Ninjago minifigures like the dragons protect the Weapons of Spinjitzu!" Sensei Wu also told me it was ok if I sent you a new Jay and told me it would be okay if I included something extra for you because anyone that saves their Christmas money to buy the Ultrasonic Raider must be a really big Ninjago fan.

So, I hope you enjoy your Jay minifigure with all his weapons. You will actually have the only Jay minifigure that combines 3 different Jays into one! I am also going to send you a bad guy for him to fight!

Just remember, what Sensei Wu said: keep your minifigures protected like the Weapons of Spinjitzu! And of course, always listen to your dad.

You will see an envelope from LEGO within the next two weeks with your new minifigures. Please take good care of them, Luka. Remember that you promised to always leave them at home.

Sincerely,
Richard
LEGO Consumer Services[1]

---

[1] https://www.babble.com/parenting/a-7-year-old-boy-lost-a-lego-figure-and-legos-customer-service-won-everything/

Richard is our hero. For us the brand lesson here is the value of amazing customer-service staff empowered to do cool things like this. Luka will be a brand fan for life. This one email was shared exponentially, creating even more fans. Branding doesn't end when Luka's dad walks out of the store with a new set; it never ends. Good branding seizes every opportunity to be awesome.

Lesson 45

Ludicrous Speed Innovation

SCOTT REALLY WANTS A TESLA; Alison has some concerns—for instance, the children who regularly muck up the Volvo we currently fight to keep clean and the fact that she often forgets to charge her phone. Anyway, we're pretty sure we'll have one someday. Probably once the mess makers are old enough to have their own cars.

It's hard not to be impressed the brand. Aside from its cars' environmentally friendly power, in itself disruptive, its designs are beautiful and Tesla is using direct-to-customer selling, foregoing the dealership model used by other car manufacturers. Founder Elon Musk believes that "franchise dealers have a fundamental conflict of interest when it comes to selling gasoline-powered cars: Traditional dealers make more money from selling services, tuneups and add-ons than they do from selling cars, while the company makes a profit from selling its electric cars. They simply cannot explain the merits of Tesla's new electric technology without undermining their traditional business at the same time." The company also uses a pre-sales model, "which was rarely used in the automotive industry before as a way to gauge the demand, because it doesn't have

126

inventory."[1] Not only is Tesla fundamentally changing the way a car is fueled and designed, it's changing the way it's sold and turning a tenet of the car industry on its head.

Even its customer service is amazing, as one entrepreneur Loic Le Meur shared on Medium:

> I was recently driving to a meeting in Silicon Valley and had to charge my Tesla. I decided to stop at the San Carlos supercharger on my way to Palo Alto and there were 5 other Tesla cars waiting in line to get a charging space. Most drivers seemed to have gone somewhere else as their cars were charging. The San Carlos supercharger is located within walking distance from Whole Foods, Peet's Coffee, a gym and some restaurants. Many drivers therefore keep their cars parked at the supercharger even once their cars have finished charging.
>
> I tweeted at Elon to tell him. Within minutes, Elon promised to take action. And then, he did.[2]

Six days later, Tesla announced on its website that they'd "designed the Supercharger network to enable a seamless, enjoyable road trip experience. Therefore, we understand that it can be frustrating to arrive at a station only to discover fully charged Tesla cars occupying all the spots. To create a better experience for all owners, we're introducing a fleet-wide idle fee that aims to increase Supercharger availability."[2]

It's beautiful in its simplicity; a customer had an issue, tweeted it to the company founder, and then within an impressive turnaround time the issue was resolved—all in public for other customers and the broader market to see.

Tesla's branding hasn't been without challenges,[3] but the lesson for us is in how it took responsibility for mistakes and then corrected them. When news spread that it had been paying outsourced workers below minimum wage, it corrected that situation. It also has a powerful understanding of

---

[1] http://digiday.com/marketing/tesla-can-do-stuff-your-brand-cannot/
[2] http://www.inc.com/justin-bariso/elon-musk-takes-customer-complaint-on-twitter-from-idea-to-execution-in-6-days.html
[3] http://adage.com/article/agency-viewpoint/brand-lessons-worst-2016/307561/

who their consumers are and an ability and a willingness to make them feel a part of a larger community.

Now, we know what you're thinking; if I was considered a visionary leader bringing a message of innovation on a global scale, I could do things like that too! There is a danger in learning from millionaires (or in this case billionaires)—from looking to those at the top of their industries and thinking "if I just do what they do, I too will be successful! I might even be able to afford a Tesla." The formative, even failed, lessons of business are much more important to learn from.

Our most valuable lesson from Tesla is that no one is born a leader—every person starts with the same number of followers and the same size community (even Elon Musk). Begin by working to position yourself as an expert by helping and sharing the knowledge you have. An accountant may not have a solution to the energy crisis to work with, but she certainly can become an expert that people look to for answers. Then when those same people need to hire an accountant, she's the obvious choice.

As an aside, while researching for *UnBranding*, Allison discovered that Tesla's new addition to the Model S sedan and Model X SUV upgrades their speed to "0 to 60 mph in 2.8 seconds, and the SUV in 3.3," and is called "Ludicrous Speed."

1. If you don't know why that's amazing, Google it. We'll wait.
2. If you don't know why that's amazing, we can't be friends.
3. Now she wants one.

Lesson 46

Kickstarter Scrappiness

FEW INNOVATIONS HAVE DISRUPTED THE business world as much as crowd-funding. Using the digital advancements of the Internet and online sharing, entrepreneurs and artists now have a new way to fund and launch their ideas. Charities all over the world can connect and collect donations to back their good works and educate people about their causes. Crowd-funding took the power away from banks and large financiers and put it in the hands of individuals who would give small amounts, all from their computers and phones. This new world promised a sum greater than the total of their donation amounts; it promised marketing and promotion and research and development. In short, crowdfunding promised community.

We've backed everything from documentary films to toys for the kids, and we've supported microloans to female entrepreneurs in Asia, all via crowdfunding sites such as Kickstarter, Indiegogo, and Kiva. As marketing speakers and authors, we've also spent lots of time answering audience questions about how to be successful in crowdfunding. Everyone wanted to take advantage of this new and developing tool. We aren't going to go into all this stuff here, so if you're new to UnMarketing or just want to learn more about our views on crowdfunding, check out:

- *The Book of Business Awesome/UnAwesome*—Chapter 23, "Part Man, Part Machine, All Crowdfunded" (the story of Detroit and its Robocop statue)
- *UnSelling*—Chapter 39, "Crowdfunding—Our Thoughts" along with actual smartness from an expert on the topic, Jason Sadler

While the Internet didn't invent people's desire to find new, unknown companies, the endless shopping options sure haven't lessened it. We all want to believe we've discovered something cool and want to be the one who tells our family and friends all about it. Crowdfunding sites count on this, creating an online marketplace of ideas just waiting to be discovered—and made possible—by you.

Terms like "small-batch," "artisanal," and "locally sourced" have all become increasingly popular on sites like Kickstarter. Because funding happens in public, these terms aren't simply catchphrases to sell to backers; they become part of our branding language as backers are encouraged to share their brand stories. Kickstarter products start branding as they gain funding, and it seems to have been so successful that now bigger brands are looking for a piece of this small-batch messaging.

The Clorox Company is one such company that with $5.8 billion in annual sales—not exactly a business in need of crowdfunding—decided to use Kickstarter to launch its new Three Jerks Jerky. According to the head of the unit responsible for the product, "One of the pillars of the strategy was trying to align our emerging brand with others in the marketplace. There's so much going on in food and beverage today, but all the interesting stuff is happening at the under-$25 million companies—all the trends, all the interesting flavors, all the interesting business models." "The idea was to help foster a mindset of running as 'entrepreneurial and scrappy, very much like the startup within the company.'"[1]

We're not sure about you, but this seems like a pretty big jerk move to us. We like to believe the companies using Kickstarter actually need

---

[1] http://adage.com/article/cmo-strategy/clorox-kickstarter-fund-venture-startup/308014/

funding and promotion rather than find we're all being tricked into believing they're "scrappy." To us, this falls to the site, which should see this as a threat to the trust it's developed over time with backers, a trust that fuels the entire ecosystem its platform is built on.

If you're thinking about using Kickstarter to generate buzz when you don't need the money, please reconsider. Our lesson here is that if you're small and scrappy, be small and scrappy, but if you're large and well-funded, spend your money on marketing because in today's digital world being fake-artisanal will come back to bite you in the jerky.

Lesson 47

When Crowdfunding Fails

As we noted in the preceding chapter, crowdfunding—and specifically Kickstarter—has been a popular tool for entrepreneurs in our innovative age. The ability to fund projects, create community, and spread the word about new, exciting products brings together social media and our access to information incredibly effectively. The megaphone of social media, however, can't discern between good news and bad news, as we'll see in our next three brand stories, which all have lessons about what not to do on Kickstarter.

Pebble

Recently, FitBit bought Pebble[1]—not in its entirety mind you, just some of the tech and staff. The rest of the product line is being shut down. This means that anyone who actually got a Pebble watch won't be able to count on updates or service going forward. Although the company did provide refunds to those who backed the Pebble 2, which is better than some failed

---

[1] http://bgr.com/2016/12/07/pebble-kickstarter-fitbit-acquisition-pebble-core/

Kickstarter users have done, they haven't exactly acted in an upstanding and trustworthy way. When things got rocky for Pebble—the company is reportedly well into debt—the founders seem to have sold off the assets quickly, forgetting about Pebble's employees and loyal customer base, and vanished off to advise other hardware startups on how not to fail.

It's hard to imagine how the company could have been in debt at all. The point of Kickstarter is to raise needed funds without acquiring debt, and the Pebble campaign, which initially sought $100,000 in backing, ended up earning a whopping $10 million—and that was just their first campaign; the second reached $20 million! With that much money in play, it's tough to believe that money was the issue for Pebble. The platform is great when money is the only thing keeping you from success, but how often is that really the case? Delays in production were blamed on "unforeseen" challenges; however, anyone who has ever managed a production run of anything can tell you there are always issues that arise. These are not unforeseen, or unexpected; they are part of business and you need to be prepared for them. The benefit of fixing these issues without the glare of attention Kickstarter can bring is incredibly valuable.

Zano Nano Drone

The Zano[2] was really cool; we actually saw it at CES a few years back, and Scott wanted 10 of them. Small enough to fit in your hand, the Zano offered mobile controls from your phone and the ability to shoot video and take images. The Kickstarter campaign looked very promising, saying that the "Zano is up and flying, holding position, avoiding obstacles, streaming live video back to a smart device, capturing video and photos," and promising that its "supply chain is 100% ready to go, from vital components that make Zano fly, to the very boxes that Zano is packaged in." Seems like everything is in order—everyone tell everyone! The campaign raised £2.3 million (US $3.5 million) and still holds the spot as the most-backed European Kickstarter project ever.

---

[2] https://medium.com/kickstarter/how-zano-raised-millions-on-kickstarter-and-left-backers-with-nearly-nothing-85c0abe4a6cb

Then the production issues began. Parts arrived late from suppliers (as they sometimes do), testing took longer than expected (as it often does), some parts arrived with issues from a manufacturer (as they periodically will), and customers who were waiting began to get grumpy (as they can from time to time). When a small first run was ready, Zano chose to ship them out to pre-order customers, rather than to Kickstarters. When people found out about this, they were angry. The pre-order customers joined them in anger, when their Zanos didn't work properly. The company filed for bankruptcy, having not only spent all the money raised but acquiring over a million more in debt.

The Coolest Cooler

Alison absolutely loved this one. For the name alone it deserved backing. The cooler had a cutting board, a Bluetooth speaker, a blender, and a charger, and it kept drinks and food cold. However, three years after the successful campaign ended, only a third of backers had received coolers. A year after the campaign, when the company started hearing from angry backers, they sent them a letter—explaining that they'd underestimated how challenging it would be to mail them a cooler. And then, they started selling the ones they had made on Amazon, "to keep the lights on" they claimed.[3] To get their coolers, the company told backers they'd have to pay an extra $97. As you can imagine, people were not pleased.

The Lessons

If you are considering backing a product on Kickstarter, please remember the platform is not a store. You are making an investment in an idea—not purchasing a product. If your investment works out, you'll get a product and be part of getting a new company off the ground. However, investments don't always work out, and you may send in your money and not receive anything. Don't invest thinking you're guaranteed anything, because you're not.

---

[3] http://mashable.com/2016/04/16/coolest-cooler-money/#pCZ7O9c5faqq

The platforms are learning lessons too, as they've become well known for their successes, as well as their failures. Kickstarter and Indiegogo have both started offering inventors access to experts in design and manufacturing. "These services include a detailed design review of electronics, global sourcing of components and manufacturing, and even assistance with branding, distribution—the kind of information that is often jealously guarded by large multinationals."[4] Both platforms have also formed relationships with partner companies, who provide audits and services to inventors.

Today, it seems even established companies have a hard time maintaining trust with their market. Businesses with products that have already been manufactured, tested, packaged, and shipped experience constant issues maintaining good faith with their market. They arrive late, they're broken, mine doesn't work the way I wanted it to—and on and on. And those are established companies. If you are considering Kickstarter, please make sure you've done some manufacturing and testing—and if you haven't be up front about this. Let backers know that part (or all) of their money is going into getting the first run complete and there will be delays and bumps along the way. This way you're setting achievable expectations and when yours is the first product in history to have an initial run with no problems, you'll exceed your promises. The more transparent you are, the less you'll have to hide later. Treat your Kickstarter campaign like an invitation you're sending out to the world, for a party they paid for.

---

[4] https://www.wired.com/2017/05/crowdfunding-platforms-crack-down-on-risky-campaigns/.

Lesson 48

Don't Make It Weird

WHEN YOU DO GREAT WORK, provide solid service, and/or create an amazing product, people talk about it. They share their experiences with your business and with friends, your family, and the world. This concept was at the heart of *UnSelling*, where we looked at the Sales Cloud and how to spread the word about your business simply by doing good work and making it easy for customers and clients to talk about it. Referrals drive new business better than any ad campaign or flashy rebranding. Simply put: we do business with people we know, like, and trust, and recommendations are the fuel behind that.

So when Andrew MacDonald[1] visited a new dentist and had a positive experience, you would think the office's work was done. A happy customer was created and sent out into the world with a good story to share with anyone looking for a new dentist. Maybe the marketer in you would like to take another step and stay in touch with Andrew. You could check in with him by phone or email or by sending a letter. You could ask him for

---

[1] https: // www.facebook.com/andrewrmacdonald/posts/1218865551478113

feedback on his experience with you to see whether improvements could be made, remind him of future appointments, or send him some useful articles about dental care—all good options. Some might even ask for referrals or for comments on Yelp for dentists. (Is there a Yelp for dentists?)

Well, Andrew's dentist had another idea! Andrew received a letter thanking him for being a patient and including a little something extra at the end—a "gift."

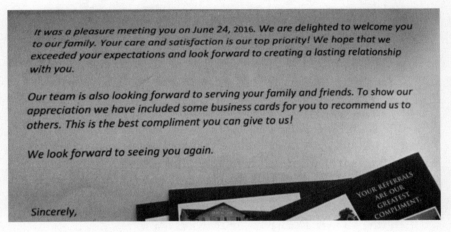

It was a pleasure meeting you on June 24, 2016. We are delighted to welcome you to our family. Your care and satisfaction is our top priority! We hope that we exceeded your expectations and look forward to creating a lasting relationship with you.

Our team is also looking forward to serving your family and friends. To show our appreciation we have included some business cards for you to recommend us to others. This is the best compliment you can give to us!

We look forward to seeing you again.

Sincerely,

Photo credit: Andrew MacDonald

To show our appreciation we have included some business cards for you to recommend us to others.

Business cards. Not a toothbrush, floss, or an appointment reminder card. Not even a handy-dandy dentist desk calendar (because who doesn't need more of those!). Business cards. We can just picture Andrew flashing his beautiful smile and handing them out at the office or at his next family dinner! We don't have a problem with asking for referrals, or even giving out business cards, but under the guise of a "gift?" Nah.

Please, we beg of you, we understand why you want referrals, but giving them out on your behalf is not a requirement or a gift you would give to your customers. Learn from Andrew's dentist: don't take a positive brand experience and make it weird.

Lesson 49

Integral Wealth Lacks Integrity

THE ETHICS AND PRACTICES BEHIND your company's hiring policies are what constitutes branding. There was a time when résumés went no further than a desk in the Human Resources department, but today they can go viral. Jeff in office 102 no longer can treat people in any way he chooses, not when his interactions can be recorded and forwarded. In the age of disruption, no part of your business is truly private, and we believe this is a good thing. We want discriminatory practices made public. We want you to know what kind of company you're applying to, and we want Jeff to be accountable. Good hiring equals good business.

The CBC (Canadian Broadcasting Company, for non-Canadians) reported this year that a man filed a complaint with the Human Rights Tribunal of Ontario after receiving a rejection email from a potential employer that mentioned Somali culture and a resistance to authority. "Jama Hagi-Yusuf was applying to jobs in the spring of 2015 when he saw a posting on Indeed.ca looking for an investment adviser's assistant with a financial company in Kitchener, which he thought was an entry-level office position.

"The University of Waterloo science grad applied, and was surprised when he received a response just hours later. But the email shocked him. The letter Hagi-Yusuf received back on May 8, 2015 read:

> I have read stories about how Somalia has a culture of resistance to authority. Such a culture would be quite different than the Canadian culture, which sees makes cutting ahead in a lineup as a great social error.
>
> The investment industry is a subculture with its own rules and traditions. It is normal for people to train for entry into this field. While your academic career suggests the training would be well within your competence, there is no demonstrated enthusiasm in past experience for entering this subculture.
>
> Due to lack of background, I must decline your application.
>
> Good luck with finding a suitable position.

The letter was signed by J. Sandy Matheson of Integral Wealth Securities Limited."[1]

The branding lesson here is to fire the "Mr. Mathesons" in your company. The digital age didn't create discrimination, but it does allow the light of your market's eyes to shine brightly on it. Human Resources is the most powerful branding division in your company. How and who you hire and how current employees are treated and supported make up the framework that builds your brand. Check your policies, discuss issues with employees, and put everything in place that you can to build a strong, diverse environment for success. When customers are registering complaints about poor service, the solution may be that you need to treat your people better.

---

[1] http://www.cbc.ca/beta/news/canada/kitchener-waterloo/job-posting-somalia-background-discrimination-1.3668307

Lesson 50

T.G.I.S' Monday

FOR A LONG TIME, THE Super Bowl ad has been the king of commercials. As Canadians, we live vicariously through our neighbors to the south who share the spots on social media. Companies spend gazillions of dollars (give or take) to create and broadcast these 30-second wonders to one of the largest television audiences in the world. These audiences have come to expect nothing less than the exceptional, forgoing our usual aversion to commercials to the point where conversations online about the ads can be on par with those about the actual game.

So this year when Kraft Heinz decided to forgo Super Bowl advertising to do something different, it caught our attention. Without any actual facts to back this up, we assume that the company could afford the spot and decided to spend the money differently by giving its entire U.S. workforce the following Monday off. The action didn't stop there. Kraft Heinz made a video about the vacation day and asked viewers to sign an online petition calling for a national holiday every Monday after Super Bowl. The Change .org petition included the video and the following call to action:

> At Heinz we believe in never settling. Never settling with food. And never settling in life.
>
> We can all agree that going to work the Monday after the "Big Game" on Sunday is awful. So as far as we're concerned at Heinz, we as a nation should stop settling for it being the worst work day of the year. We don't settle for that awesome football Sunday to be just like every other day of the year. No. We eat. We drink. And we be merry, having the tastiest times of our lives. But then the very next day we settle for that Monday being a terrible work day.
>
> Statistics show over 16 million people call in sick or just don't show up to work. And for those that do, productivity plummets so far that the country loses on average around $1 billion (true story). Enough with the madness. This is where YOU come in.
>
> Sign the petition to make the day after the Big Game a National Holiday. Share it with friends, family and even strangers and get THEM to sign it. If we get over 100,000 signatures, it will be sent to Congress.
>
> If we can make Big Game Sunday awesome, we can make the Monday after awesome too. Make that Monday more like Sunday. Make it a SMUNDAY and have more Sunday on your Monday than any of us have ever had in our lives. Don't settle. Sign it. For your sanity. For your family. For your country.[1]

We've never felt so good about our food purchases before.

As a brand lesson, we ask you to consider that just because you've always done something, or all the big companies are doing it, or it's the most expensive option, or because your ego thinks it would be nice doesn't mean you should automatically chose it. No action will automatically lead to success; we need to be thinking creatively, and sometimes that means not doing what seems like the most obvious choice.

---

[1] http://bgr.com/2017/01/26/kraft-heinz-super-bowl-holiday-petition/

Lesson 51

When Everything Goes Up in Flames

LOGISTICS IS A CHALLENGE many entrepreneurs overlook when they're starting out. We spend so much energy getting products ready to go, creating beautiful websites, investing in marketing and social media. We open bank accounts and lines of credit and sort out our invoicing and stock managements. And then once all the boxes are checked and orders begin to come in we realize we forgot to factor in the additional cost and time of putting orders together, packing them efficiently, and actually getting them to our customers' doorsteps. In the age where free shipping has become the expectation, we learn all too quickly that UPS does not share this ideal and would actually like, and in fact requires us to pay them.

Logistics is a beast of a task. First of all, we need to find and acquire boxes and labels. Just when we thought our design work was over, we need to decide whether we design something cool, or on brand, to add to the shopping experience. When Alison was just getting Nummies off the ground, she realized by her fourth sales trip that not all stores were equipped to sell bras hung on hangers as she'd assumed they could. The majority of her customers ended up being baby-product retailers who wanted items in pretty boxes. Customers wanted to be able to see and touch the products. Service staff didn't want to spend all of their time unboxing and reboxing. And so began weeks of searching and work on packaging, which ended up to be expensive and time consuming.

Then we have packing and shipping. For the entrepreneur, this can mean glamorous late hours taping boxes and visits back and forth to the post office, all time that may not have been calculated into the product cost. Assuming you've got your packaging sorted and you've mastered the art of shipping, your product then goes out into the world of the post office, which can be a bumpy place as we learned from our next brand story.

The Be Bangles people had done everything right. It was before the holiday season, and they'd fulfilled and shipped 80 orders, about $6,000 worth of business. This is where entrepreneurs should be able to give themselves a pat on the back and move on to the next task at hand. However, this wasn't to be the case. The next day they were contacted by a firefighter, who notified them that someone had set fire to the mailbox they'd used, which unfortunately contained their packages. They contacted the post office with questions and began damage control. Just how much damage had been done? What kind of damage? When and where could they collect their items? Was there anything left to collect?

> On the first call they told us they had no record of a fire, and even if there was a fire all they could do was send us 10 stamps to replace what we'd lost.[1]

We're not sure 10 stamps is going to cover this.

The post office went on to assure them that damaged packages would not be sent out, because the only thing more likely to anger their customers than late holiday gifts would be burnt late holiday gifts. They were

---

[1] https://bebangles.co/blogs/blog/someone-set-a-post-office-box-on-fire-and-australia-post-sent-the-burnt-remains-to-our-customers

promised a call-back in a few days, but this call never happened. They tried to visit the post office depot in person, and were told it was not open to the public. And then they got these emails:

> "Uh Hi, this may sound odd, but I've just received my bangles in the mail—and they look like they've been burned?"

> "In all years I've been receiving mail never has this happened! So upset!"

> "It's really strange—everything seems waterlogged and also smells of smoke. It's almost like the post box was set on fire and put out with water (I have a vivid imagination)."

> "Hi, I just received my order and strangely it has been on fire at some point."

> "As you can see in the photo, the envelope must have somehow caught fire and then soaked. The little pouches were still wet and had become moldy. Not sure what the hell happened at Australia Post that day!"

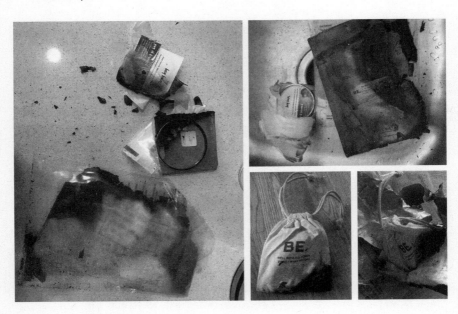

Photo credit: Jesse Newton

One customer even had a note with the package from the Australian Post blaming the damage on poor packaging by the company.

The Be Bangles people did the only thing they could. They reached out and apologized to every customer and sent out new product as soon as possible. They told the story on their blog, and when it went viral they offered anyone reading a discount, with the code "firesale." When we reached out to Be Bangles Director of Operations Lauren Markwell to ask permission to share the story, she wrote, "After the blog post went viral we ended up getting a lot of media, and Australia Post ended up compensating us for the damages. We believe that without the public profile of the story they never would have done anything, so we are so incredibly grateful for that. We even got a lot of people ordering bangles purely to support us after they saw the story on the news. How great is that for supporting your local small business!"

We absolutely adore this. When we're in the middle of a crisis as a business, sometimes we only have enough time to react, and we rarely see the opportunities within for positive change and developments. When this happens, we want you to remember Ms. Markwell's words and take every challenge as an opportunity—use her hindsight to guide your actions.

The branding lesson here is that some things you can't plan for and you need to be prepared to manage the unknown. Back up your customer lists, inventory, and all digital information so you can access these in case your computer system goes down, or your product goes up in flames. Leave space in your budget for the unknown and factor this into your costs so when the time comes you can survive. And remember, you can't change the fact that the spotlight is on your company for something negative, but you can use these setbacks as opportunities to shine. When it hits the fan, it's not time to hide behind the fan. It's time to be awesome.

Lesson 52

Sears and Our Right-Handed Chair

WE BOUGHT A CHAIR AT Sears this year for our anniversary. Alison is actually sitting in it right now writing these words. It's a chaise longue—you know the style, long and comfy with a single armrest. We'd never bought anything major there before, but while wandering through looking for something else, we saw the style of chair we wanted and placed the order. It was a custom piece so we booked a delivery time six weeks out (at no additional charge) and paid in full. We included an insurance plan, because the furniture in our house needs that kind of thing.

Six weeks later, the day had arrived and we were all set. A third-party delivery company arrived and less than happily brought the chair up to our bedroom. The delivery men left the chair wrapped up and handed Alison a piece of paper.

Delivery person: "Please sign here, Ms. Stratten, and check off these boxes."

Alison looked at the paper and there were some initialing to be done to guarantee we had the right chair. Only problem was, it was all wrapped up.

Alison: "I can't sign this because I haven't seen the chair. Can you please unwrap it or wait until I can?"

Delivery person: "You just need to sign it."

Alison: "No."

So they unwrapped the chair. Alison signed the paper and they left. All was well in the world—until Scott came to see the chair and realized something was very wrong.

Scott: "Didn't we order a right armrest? This chair has it on the left."

We'd ordered the chair with a right armrest because Scott needs it on that side for his bad shoulder—a pretty important part of the whole "custom chair" decision. So Alison called Sears and spoke to the salesperson we'd initially ordered from.

Salesperson: "That is a right-side chair. That's what you ordered."

Alison: "But the arm is on the left side and when we bought it we clearly said we needed it on the right side. We even sat in the chair and showed you exactly what we needed."

Salesperson: "That's how chairs work. It's right sided because when you look at it straight on, the arm is on the right side."

Alison: "No."

It seemed to us one would judge a chair not by how it looks facing it but how it is when actually sitting in it.

Salesperson: "Well, we can take back the chair and get you another one. Or you can keep that one and we will give you a 25% discount back on your Sears card."

Alison: "We don't have or want a Sears card. Please come and get the chair and we'll order a new one."

Salesperson: "Why don't you keep the chair until the new one is ready? It will be six weeks. Just keep it as is and we'll pick it up then"

Alison: "I don't think you've met our children/dogs/cats/us. I can't possibly promise to keep this chair brand new for six weeks. Please come and get the chair and order another one."

Salesperson: "Ok, I will just need your credit card to charge you for the second chair."

Alison: "You're going to charge me again? What about this chair?"

Salesperson: "Yes, that's our policy. We can credit you for the first chair after we charge for the second. It will take a few days."

Alison: "No. Come and get this chair, give me a refund, which only takes a minute and then order us a right-sided arm chair. Not right when you look at it, right when you sit in it."

Salesperson: "Ok."

And they did. Six weeks later, our second, new, right-sided when you sit in it, chair arrived. So much for policy I guess. Or common sense it seems.

Sears has taught us many branding lessons. Delivery staff aren't just labor—they are a part of the company's brand. We understand you're outsourcing delivery, but when our money went to Sears, our customer service is coming through Sears and the product says Sears on the box; it's all Sears. Customers don't see funnels, and all points of contact with your business are part of your brand. Don't say "policy" as an excuse for what you feel like doing at the time and then back-pedal immediately when asked. Few things anger an already frustrated customer like the word "policy." There is always something you can do; at the very least listen and be empathetic.

Don't act as if you've been put out when a customer wants to make sure they're getting what they paid for. Service is part of the job description in business—every job description. If your market is humans, you're eventually going to need to speak to one of them. Branding doesn't end with the sale, it ends when the customer decides it's over.

Lesson 53

Branding through Service

RECENTLY, THE AUTOMOBILE INDUSTRY WAS SHAKEN by the Volkswagen emissions scandal. For those of you not familiar with what happened, here's the short version.

In September 2015, the U.S. Environmental Protection Agency discovered and made public that many Volkswagen cars sold in the United States had a "defeat device—or software—in diesel engines that could detect when they were being tested, changing the performance accordingly to improve results. The German car giant has since admitted cheating emissions tests in the US."[1] The company had been marketing these cars as environmentally responsible choices without any compromise in performance. The cheat affected about 11 million cars worldwide.

Horrible, right? Unthinkable.

The branding lesson—to build a successful brand in the age of disruption don't totally misrepresent yourself and your product and don't knowingly cheat government rules and legislation or lie to all your customers and the public while destroying the planet—seems pretty obvious to us. If you're on

---

[1] http://www.bbc.com/news/business-34324772

the fence about this one, or in any way not getting that what they did should be placed in all caps on your "what not to do" list, we probably can't help you here. There's no amount of good service, no flashy ad campaign or engagement on social media that can fix this.

In terms of cost, a car is one of the larger purchases we make and therefore a big commitment to a product and to a company. A car can become part of our identity, as we align ourselves with a brand in a visible way. Inherent in the purchase is a trust gap that appears when we decide this car will keep us and our loved ones safe on the road. Automakers are one of the largest advertising buyers around, with flashy commercials and even investments in racing teams to impress us. All our loyalty factors figure in the car business: cost, comfort, convenience, and convergence.

When we asked UnMarketing Facebook fans about branding and their experiences with car makers, the Volkswagen scandal came up quite a lot, as you'd likely expect. What was surprising to us, and we feel more applicable to you, were the lessons from other car makers. Unexpectedly, these stories weren't about the products but were universally about service.[2]

Here is one from Michaela Alexis:

My car dealership Donnelly Ford Lincoln! When I bought my car, they misquoted the payment amounts, screwed up my service appointment date, and were just generally super unprofessional. I promised I'd never buy from them again. THEN, I brought my car in for a repair a month ago, and they were AMAZING! I felt taken care of, and not only did the mechanic fix my dual clutch, the dude VACUUMED my car, put all my shoes in a box in the trunk, my mugs in another box in the trunk (don't judge me:)), AND left a beautiful handwritten card on my steering wheel with some Donnelly swag. Now I can't even imagine buying elsewhere!

Nadine Bellhouse wrote:

Honda: Huge race car fans and owned a Civic an Acura and a mini van. Then one day we got a letter that our van might potentially have

[2] https://www.facebook.com/UnMarketing/posts/10155288147715942

an engine failure issue. When we brought it to the dealership they told us that it was past the warranty mileage and would not fix it even though they acknowledged that it was a factory failure/recall issue! We had been customers of that dealership for 10+ years. Even wrote a letter to the president of Honda Canada. Too bad so sad they said. So did I, went to GM and have been loyal ever since.

We can come up with a few explanations as to why service is the key to car branding success. As we wrote in *UnSelling*, today most purchase decisions are made before a person ever enters your funnel. Buyers are armed with so much information before ever stepping into a dealership, they've likely decided which car they're going to buy on their own. A salesperson can certainly affect the decision or create opportunities for added features, but the basic choice walks in with the customer. That's why most of our branding stories weren't about the car underperforming or not meeting expectations, because the customers knew what they wanted and what to expect from the car.

Now the service department is more of a wild card. It's not made up of metal parts and heated seats; the service department is humans, and humans are unpredictable and subject to change. This leaves service open to much more variety in experience. Dealerships actually make little money on the cars themselves; the money is to be made in financing loans, upgrades, and of course, years of service. That's the lesson from car dealerships: product is nice, but service is key.

Lesson 54

#GoForTheLawsuit

THE OLYMPICS IS ONE OF the most recognizable brands in the world. The rings logo is iconic, and each host city invests a fortune creating its own special take on the games—bringing together their own identity and culture to welcome the world to their home. As many of us do with our own hard-built brands, the Olympics committee is protective and concerned about others stealing and/or profiting off them. The thing is, when your brand is an event you invite the whole world to—they tend to show up and excitedly want to share their experiences. We see this same struggle with artists locking down phones at concerts, trying to prevent rogue videos.

Attempting to lock down social media is pretty much impossible in a world where everyone has a phone in their pocket. Brands were used to being able to control the message, only sending out content they'd written and approved, but today the content comes from everyone. Trying to lock it down can anger fans who want to be able to share their lives with the world. We pay for ad campaigns, we even pay influencers to share our stories, but when the content is free and uncontrolled we become nervous. Brands become defensive, creating barriers to people sharing their content.

Before the Olympic Games held in Rio de Janeiro in 2016, the Olympic committee decided to try and lock things down by treating their hashtag like a trademark. The thing is, a hashtag is not a trademark, it's simply a way to make searching for your content easier. It can be copied, and when things go wrong, hijacked.

The Olympic Committee sent out an official warning to companies telling them they weren't permitted to tweet any content related to the games, unless they were official sponsors in partnership with the organization.[1] This included sponsors of individual athletes. The letter explicitly warned these companies that they were forbidden from using any phrases that had been trademarked by the United States Olympic Committee (USOC), including such popular terms as "Olympic," "Olympian," and "Go for the gold," along with many other phrases usually used to describe the international sporting event. The warnings went on to include referencing event results and using images taken at the event.

The lockdown was made worse by news coming out of the Olympic village that things weren't exactly up to standard for the athletes. Teams were reporting online that buildings were uninhabitable and unsafe. These athletes rely on individual sponsorships offered by the very businesses and community groups who were being warned about sharing news coming out of the games. Without these sponsorships, many athletes couldn't afford to train and compete. Not only were the athletes living in subpar conditions, but their supporters were being put on social media lockdown.

There are few brands as established as the Olympics, and as a branding teacher for disruption, few can compare. The games were born not only before the Internet but before television. As your office has been struggling with a few new staff under 40 and how to optimize diversity in the workplace, the Olympics continually welcomes young athletes and fans from around the world. As we watched the outrage unfold over the games,

---

[1] http://www.ibtimes.co.uk/olympics-committee-bans-non-sponsors-tweeting-about-rio-2016-games-1573029

we wondered how they would make it through; then we remembered the brand had also survived two actual wars.

The brand lesson here is you can't control the conversation. To continue to survive the ups and downs of change and digital innovation, the Olympics will need to evolve and come to understand that today "PR" no longer stands for "public relations" or "press release"; it stands for "people react." You can't control the reaction and you can't control how we all share common events and experiences online. Instead of spending time and energy trying to control the conversation, focus on providing good stories to share and watch them spread.

Lesson 55

Wells Fargo and Why Elizabeth Warren Is Our Hero

WE DO MOST OF OUR BANKING in person. Over the years we've found it just makes things easier to know the branch employees and take the time to stop in for face-to-face contact. There is a huge trust gap involved in bank branding; you leave them all your money and trust they know what they're doing. They're part of your largest purchases, including your home, and often they're the first stop for the would-be entrepreneur. So when banks break this trust, there's an understandable ripple effect.

Wells Fargo came under a lot of scrutiny when it was charged with fraud and forced to pay $185 million. Rather than take any responsibility, their CEO John Stumpf passed the buck to front-line staff, blaming them for opening millions of fake bank and credit card accounts, all the while billing customers for services they never asked for. Although employees claimed they were forced into these unethical choices by a "pressure-cooker sales culture," Mr. Stumpf fired over 5,000 workers for what he described as not honoring the bank's culture.[1] After the court battle, Wells Fargo changed tactics and saw a pretty dramatic and expected decrease in sales, although more recently the numbers seem to be going back up to normal.[2]

It can be challenging to figure out the reasons behind all of this. We've had this debate before—Brand A cheats, lies, and is generally horrible, and all this is made public. There's some short-lived online outrage, and then the crowd moves on to the next thing. Brand A recovers, and life goes on. So what's the lesson here? It can't be that "all press is good press." The answer is that our brand choices are made for a series of reasons and rarely in a straight line.

A brand cheating its customers cannot possibly be good for business. As we wrote in *UnSelling*, we need to look at the Brand Pulse. With each interaction, positive or negative, the needle is moved. When it's down, we're more susceptible to competition, and when it's up, we're more likely to share good stories. We also need to consider all the factors, and each individual decides which factors are the most important to him or her. We may hate using a certain airline, but if they're the only one with a direct flight at the time we need, they're getting our business. Now if the airline offended a sensibility we had that was more important to us than flight patterns, we'd leave.

When U.S. Senator Elizabeth Warren faced off with Mr. Stumpf at a Senate Banking Committee hearing she referred to his company's wrongdoings as a "scam" and told him he should resign and face a criminal investigation. She began her questioning by citing Wells Fargo's Vision and Values Statement, particularly its suggestion "If you want to find out how strong a company's ethics are, don't listen to what its people say, watch what they do." She also called out the high-pressure sales as a way to falsely inflate stock prices, saying, "'In all 12 of these calls, you personally cited Wells Fargo's success at cross-selling retail accounts as one of the main reasons to buy more stock in the company.'" She went on to condemn Stumpf's lack of personal responsibility, saying, "'And when

---

[1] http://www.huffingtonpost.com/entry/john-stumpf-wells-fargo_us_57d87d54e4b0fbd4b7bc4c85
[2] https://consumerist.com/2017/02/17/wells-fargos-new-account-openings-down-30-after-fake-account-fiasco/

it all blew up, you kept your job, you kept your multi-multimillion-dollar bonuses, and you went on television to blame thousands of $12-an-hour employees who were just trying to meet cross-sell quotas that made you rich.'"[3]

What lessons can we learn from Wells Fargo? Here's the list:

- Elizabeth Warren is our hero.
- Putting undue pressure on your sales team can lead to fraud.
- We all need to be careful choosing companies with which to trust our hard-earned money.
- The bottom line should not and cannot be the guiding factor when making business choices.

Not all press is good for your brand.

---

[3] http://www.npr.org/sections/thetwo-way/2016/09/20/494738797/you-should-resign-watch-sen-elizabeth-warren-grill-wells-fargo-ceo-john-stumpf

Lesson 56

The Secret to Going Viral

MOST OF US UNDERSTAND THAT brand awareness is a crucial part of branding. If no one knows about your brand, does it even exist? Getting the word out in this new world is different from what it used to be. It's no longer about the size of your ad-spend budget but rather how much of a mindshare we can capture in the fleeting world of newsfeeds (and BuzzFeed). There's no argument that creating content that resonates is the key. Scott has always said, "Make great content and you'll get the views/likes/subscribers you were hoping for."

Today, it's no longer enough to focus on content alone. It's still key, but focusing on the content's context is also hugely important; how and where people are consuming the content, why they think they should be consuming it, and how they were referred to it cannot be overlooked. We have the UnScientific proof.

Last year, we shared a clip of Scott's "Millennial Rant" on the UnMarketing Facebook page. Because we know that 85% of videos are watched with the sound off we added closed-captioning, so people could see the words he was yelling from on stage.[1]

UnMarketing ✓
Published by Scott Stratten [?] · January 9 · ⊙

What we mean when we say "Millennials".

We sent the clip out to just under 50,000 "fans" and it did great, quickly reaching over 250,000 "views."

That's a solid number for anything on Facebook, since the average reach of a brand post is pretty pitiful.[2] But Scott knew it could do better. We've seen humor clips on Facebook, many of which weren't even that funny, reach views in the tens of millions, and we knew this clip was gold. This wasn't only arrogance talking. We know that Scott is hilarious and that this particular bit of content had been shared on stages in front of thousands of people and always killed—they laugh, hard.

From the initial data, we found the video would do well with immediate fans, and then drop off—there just wasn't enough there to entice people not directly connected to UnMarketing to watch, so Scott had the team at Atomic Spark Video add a text title bar and rereleased it.

---

[1] http://digiday.com/media/silent-world-facebook-video/

[2] http://marketingland.com/facebook-organic-reach-drop-steepens-52-publishers-pages-187253

And KABOOM! It received over 14,000,000 views, and counting.

The title had to be something engaging enough for people to stop and watch, even if they had no previous connection to us. Headline writing is an art, and a good headline can make the difference between your content being opened or being totally ignored; for us, this was the 250,000 to 14 million view difference. A word of caution here—headline writing is something that can tread into the skeezy, click bait world of "Woman Puts Hand In Blender, YOU WON'T BELIEVE WHAT HAPPENS NEXT!" You may be able to fool someone once with a headline like that, but it's not the way to build a trusting, loyal audience.

There's a lot to learn from the Millennial video and why it took off—a classic case of Second Circle Evaporation. In the *Book of Business Awesome/UnAwesome*, we use the concept of "third circle" to explain how online content goes viral.

You and your brand's Facebook page are in the middle of the circle. From here, you share a post with your first circle, fans and friends of your brand. These are people who know you and your content and want to see it. A small selection of this first circle will see any given post and decide

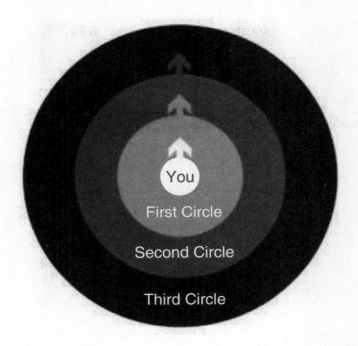

whether to pass it along—to like, share, and/or comment on. If they do, this exposes the post to their own first circle, which is your second circle.

The people in the second circle have no direct relationship to you or your brand, and they're much harder to reach and to impress. This is where most content dies; with no established brand connection, the second circle will rarely pass your content along. This is what happened to the first posting of the Millennial video.

When Scott added the headline, it was enough to stop the second circle scroll. Once they'd watched even a few seconds, we had them. Then the content did its magic; they loved it even with no previous brand connection, and away it went! This is the third circle, and the true meaning of something going viral. The most important lesson for viral content is: If the content isn't good, third circle doesn't happen; it's the combination of grabbing attention with a strong (and not misleading) headline, combined with a great video, that makes the viral happen.

Lesson 57

Cookies and Apple

WE COUNTED.

One desktop, one laptop (a beloved MacBook Air, typing this very book), three Apple TVs (seriously, could the remote be harder to find?), four phones used as phones, one phone used as an iPod (music only; kids get phones when they graduate from grade eight around here), four iPads, and one iPod. These are just the ones we actively use. There are a bunch of old phones and iPods in drawers around the house. We aren't sure why we save them all, but anyway, it's clear we love us some Apple.

Just this morning, the kids were texting Alison "Ice Ice Baby" lyrics so she could hear Siri read them. That's fun for the whole iFamily.

Why do we love Apple? Let us count the ways.

1. *Warranty and locations nearby and wherever we travel.* Alison has needed to replace a phone in New York (dropped from her jeans pocket into the toilet), a phone in Orlando (dropped from our balcony into a field of zebras at Disney's Animal Kingdom), and a laptop in Las Vegas (died containing the only copy of *The Book of Business Awesome*). Alison breaks things—a lot.

2. *Family sharing.* We buy most of our music, movies, and TV shows on one account, and then everyone can share seamlessly. That's why Scott has all those Barbie movies on his account, really it is.
3. *Tech knowledge.* As we've mentioned before, Scott needed to be able to speak intelligently about tech and app development at conferences, and for us this meant knowing Apple.

We also love how Apple products look and feel, how they work, and of course, the customer service.

Now as much as she loves Apple, Alison hates candles. It's mostly based in her anxiety around a child or dog or cat accidentally knocking the candle off whatever table or shelf it's on and setting the house on fire. Also, her mom used to light candles that smelled like cookies, and then there were no cookies. Candles are why she has trust issues.

Perhaps the only thing worse than teasing her about cookies might be teasing about a new Mac.

The Apple accessory company Twelve South has released a candle that smells like a brand new Apple computer.[1] You can buy the candle for $24, a small price to pay for those of us who love that new Mac smell— without the new Mac price. It's perfect for that romantic candle-light dinner, where you can each stare at your phones and pretend you're in the Apple store.

We aren't entirely sure what our lesson is here for brands. Perhaps that your goal should be to have a brand so successful that people would pay their hard-earned dollars just to smell like it. Perhaps we should take a branding lesson from new cars, Las Vegas casinos, and Apple and remember to delight all our customers' senses, from the scent of your locations to the music you play, to make the whole experience as memorable and comfortable as possible.

We wonder what the UnMarketing candle would smell like. Probably conference hall coffee or a crisp new book. Most likely, kids, dogs, and cats. The KiDoCat UnCandle! Kickstarter campaign launching soon!

---

[1] https://consumerist.com/2016/10/04/candle-claims-to-offer-that-new-mac-smell-without-the-new-mac-price/

Lesson 58

Ad UnBlock

ONE OF THE PROBLEMS with focusing your marketing spend on traditional push types of media is that as quickly as new platforms are born, so are the ways in which we use digital innovation to block ads. In a print newspaper or magazine, we had no choice but to see your ad, but online tools such as AdBlock Plus quickly developed to keep those pesky images off our screens. The issue is that ad dollars keep media outlets afloat. So we find ourselves in the tug of war between seeing ads and doing everything we can to block them.

AdBlock Plus made a name for itself as a plugin that kept pesky ads from your desktops.[1] The service reviewed ads sent in by publishers and let only those deemed "acceptable" through its filter, with about 30% making the cut.

Recently, however, the company started selling ads of its own, which depending on how you look at things, is either a logical step as it grows or a complete reversal of its previous brand message. For users, the experience of using AdBlock Plus will likely not change in any noticeable way. However,

---

[1] https://consumerist.com/2016/09/13/adblock-plus-goes-into-the-business-of-selling-ads-wait-what/

from a branding perspective this departure may interfere with the strength of what it's known for. They aren't called AdLetSomeOfThemInEr . . .

For your brand, the lesson here is about branding over time. When you're getting started the strength of a clear brand voice it critical, but this is true over time as well. Change is unavoidable and even desirable, but how you manage and communicate that change will affect how your brand is viewed over time. Here, transparency is key. As long as AdBlock Plus is being clear about what it does, users will understand and move forward. On the other hand, a brand that changes without sharing this information publically, clearly, and upfront can find itself outed—chasing after the message it no longer controls.

Lesson 59

The Definition of Awesome

OFTEN IN BRANDING WE HAVE product envy; struggling to come up with a creative new way to share our product, we look enviously at other companies and dream of having something that exciting to sell. If only we made laptops, or makeup, or beautiful furniture—then we too could have a popular brand. We see this all over, from financial companies to toilet paper; the grass is always greener on the other side of the shopping street.

So if we had to guess what brand would make a name for itself on social media in 2017, a dictionary would not have made our top 10. What could be less innovative and flashy than a dictionary, right?

Wrong.

The year is 2017, and the resistance is being led by a dictionary. Merriam-Webster's Twitter account became a delight in the months leading up to and following the election. It subtweets President Donald Trump and his administration; it wryly speaks truth to power through cold, hard vocabulary. For example, when Trump aide Kellyanne Conway mentioned "alternative facts,"[1] Merriam-Webster tweeted out a link to a post defining "fact."

---

[1] https://www.merriam-webster.com/news-trend-watch/conway-alternative-facts-20170122

Merriam-Webster says they aren't being purposefully political, but simply reacting to search volume for certain words, which coincidentally seem to be related to the election. For example, they tweeted the definition of a "claque" when people were accusing Trump of hiring people to provide positive reactions at his speeches. Whatever the reason, the results have been entertaining and right on brand, and they have brought a lot of traffic to the dictionary's site. Our brand lesson here is not to let your industry or your history be an excuse not to be awesome. Brand envy is a waste of time; focus your attention on what makes you and your product valuable.

We look forward to 2020, when "UnMarketing" is added to the dictionary. Definition: marketing for good, with extra snark.

Lesson 60

A Degree in Community

THERE ARE SOME ICONIC BUSINESS success stories about entrepreneurs who didn't go to college. While some will tell you to forgo the whole expensive, time-consuming process, we are not those people. It's not only because we believe college to be the best choice for our children (who we hope one day will stumble upon this book and read it), it's not only because we both went ourselves (between us we have two university degrees and one college diploma—don't ask for transcripts), and it's not because Scott taught Human Resources at our local community college. We think a college education is important because it offers two invaluable things—opportunity and time.

The college opportunity factor isn't just about the piece of paper that may or may not help you land that first job. College provides the opportunity to meet and connect with a new, usually more diverse population than you find in high school. Your future business partners, vendors, and colleagues may be sitting in the lecture beside you. College gives students the opportunity to learn new information from those more experienced and to improve teamwork, time-management, and task-completion skills. For some, it's the first time they'll live independently and in a generally more secure environment, with few of the adult demands life has to offer (partners, kids, mortgages, loans, etc.). Ideally, college years are a bridge into the world of responsibility and freedom.

The time factor that some see as a disadvantage we see as a plus. If you have the resources to make it happen, why not spend a few extra years figuring out what you want to do with your life? There are very few other times when we have the chance to truly focus on what we want, and college can provide this time. What some see as time wasted, we see as time earned.

So kids, if you're reading this, that's why you're going to college. And yes, we know Steve Jobs didn't graduate, nor did Bill Gates or Oprah or Ted Turner. So did a lot of other people you've never heard of.

Higher education has had a bumpy ride through the age of disruption. On one hand, digital tools allow endless resources. Innovation has created opportunities for greater access to education through online courses and endless points of contact for communication and collaboration. As described on Purdue University's website, "Students in a classroom in the rural U.S., for example, can learn about the Arctic by following the expedition of a team of scientists in the region, read scientists' blog posting, view photos, e-mail questions to the scientists, and even talk live with the scientists via a videoconference. Students can share what they are learning with students in other classrooms in other states who are tracking the same expedition. Students can collaborate on group projects using technology-based tools such as wikis and Google docs. The walls of the classrooms are no longer a barrier as technology enables new ways of learning, communicating, and working collaboratively." The text goes on to describe the change in the role of the teacher from "sage on the stage" to "guide on the side."[1]

Rather than dictating and lecturing, the professor is there to disseminate information and guide students through the educational process. This is a critical piece of value in education, as students move into the adult world where knowing how to sort through endless information critically, is invaluable. Scott Skypes in to college classrooms using one of our books as

---

[1] http://online.purdue.edu/ldt/learning-design-technology/resources/how-has-technology-changed-education

a textbook all the time. It's one of his favorite way to connect with readers and see how students are learning from our work.

As in other industries, digital innovations have empowered education consumers—students—to share their experiences. When we were choosing schools, we had only an annual magazine rating to look toward; now there are online reviews for everything from classes, professors, housing, and even meal plans—and university president Twitter accounts of course.

When a snowstorm hit the University of Kentucky campus, students went online to share their snow stories, and Devan Dannelly, @DADannelly11 on Twitter, decided to see if he could get out of class the next day.

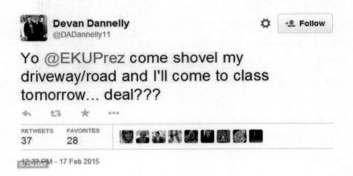

If you're the president of a large university and one of your students tweets this to you, what do you do? You could certainly ignore him, or maybe you have an automated reply for all tweets to you, something like, "Thank you for reaching out, please call the Office of the President at . . ." Well, Michael Benson decided to go a different way.

Great, right? The thing is, he didn't just reply. He went, shoveled the snow, and posted a picture of him with Devan's mom!

Seriously, how awesome is that dog!?

True to his word, and with proof in hand, Devan didn't have much choice. He showed up at class the next day as promised and shared some proof of his own.

We absolutely love this story. We love it because President Benson is fun and kind and takes the time to connect with his students. We love it because he uses Twitter to reply and shows Devan that he is valued as a student, as part of the college community, and as a person. This wasn't a community building campaign, or a one-time thing. Mr. Benson's Twitter feed is full of amazing photos of him with happy students who are excited to meet him. The best part of the story is how it inspired others to connect and help one another.

Michael Benson
@EKUPrez

🐦 Follow

Huge shout out to @EKUFootball & @KDDeltaOmicron for pitching in, shoveling walks, and digging out cars. @EKUStories

3:38 PM - 18 Feb 2015 · Richmond, KY

↰   ⇄ 18   ♥ 65

Someone in Mr. Benson's position usually has a lot of gatekeepers between him and his students, and in our experience those gatekeepers are there for a really good reason. If your CEO or dean is used to being able to say whatever he or she wants—no matter how offensive—then giving them access to a platform as reactionary as Twitter is probably not a good idea. In fact, don't let them answer the phone either or talk to people.

When Scott reached out to Mr. Benson to ask him how he manages social media in such a refreshing way, Mr. Benson replied that "they were there to serve the students." This is our lesson here—leadership as service, in the truest sense of the word, is immeasurably valuable. It fosters community within your organization, creates loyalty, and defines your brand. With Mr. Benson, we see the potential for Twitter to facilitate community and to share this community with others. By speaking to students respectfully and getting out and meeting them (and their moms and awesome dogs) he sets a wonderful example of what school leadership should look like. This is the kind of school we would have wanted to go to and the kind of school we want for our children.

Lesson 61

Pepsi Cause Jacking

THE ONLINE MEGAPHONE HASN'T ONLY opened your business practices up to the world—it's also opened up your charitable ones. Many consumers care about whether they're buying from a company that treats its employees well, and they also care about how they're giving back. A study by Omnicom Group's Cone Communications shows that 70 percent of millennials "will spend more on brands that support causes—and with millennials representing $2.45 trillion in spending power, the subject of corporate social responsibility carries an unexpected level of clout."[1]

That's a whole lot of spending dollars.

Congruency is one of our four loyalty factors, and the causes you support as a business can be one of the ways consumers decide if they think like you do. So as a business, what do you do—donate 10% of all proceeds, support a local community group, use causes in your advertising? We faced this challenge at UnMarketing when we started making jackass-whisperer socks and mugs for the *UnPodcast*—something we'll talk about more in

---

[1] http://www.adweek.com/brand-marketing/agencies-are-carving-out-niche-socially-responsible-marketing-168592/

Lesson 83, "That Week We Sold Socks." We made them to give away to listeners (and because we've always wanted jackass-whisperer socks and mugs), but when a bunch of community members started asking to buy them, we put them up for sale as well. They weren't exactly a money-making venture, but the cost paid for shipping and packaging and helped cover the expense of the ones we were giving away. Most of the feedback was positive, but we had a few people step forward to tell us that we should be giving away some (if not all) of the money to charity.

As with free shipping, it seemed the market was conditioned to expect a donation.

Even with the feedback, we didn't add a charity component to the socks and mugs, and here's why. We donate to a number of causes on a regular basis (Scott would actually give all of our money away if left to his own devices, but Alison is funny about food and shelter and education for our kids), but we do so privately. And that's our choice to make. We love and support companies that give back, but believe in their choice to do so as they wish and then live with the branding consequences. Could we have sold more socks if we'd made a public donation from each one? Possibly. But for us, this particular product wasn't going to be part of our social responsibilities, and we weren't looking to align them with any cause other than the happiness they'd bring to wearers in cubicles and open-concept offices around the world.

We saw cause marketing backfire rather spectacularly for PepsiCo this past year when the brand featured a commercial in which Kendall Jenner de-escalated police violence at a protest—with a Pepsi. Now we hope that most of us can agree that violence is bad and being thirsty is also kind of bad, but the ad was extremely offensive to many, and the uproar online led to the commercial being taken down and the company apologizing. So what went wrong? Well, the ad was clearly oversimplifying a serious issue by showing a product as the solution for violence. The timing of the ad was awful, considering how many instances of police brutality had been in the news around that time. Possibly most important, the message was empty, considering the brand hadn't come out against violence previously.

Compare Pepsi's marketing with that of Urban Outfitters, for example. After a transgender customer complained online about being kept from using one of their changing rooms, the company did more than apologize. They took a public stand on the issue, stating that they "do not endorse any laws that discriminate against the LGBTQ community, and we have supported charities that are actively fighting the anti-LGBTQ HB-2 law in North Carolina."[2] The company now actively promotes all-gender changing rooms, demonstrating a congruence with their market, based on a cause-based stance. This is what was lacking for Pepsi, whose message rang flat and offended those who were truly fighting for the cause the product company used purely for marketing purposes.

Our lesson from Pepsi and our jackass socks is that seeking congruence through social responsibility can also backfire. For every cause you support (or chose not to), there will be some who are offended. Taking a stand can be polarizing, which is why we think it shouldn't be motivated by your bottom line. If a cause is one you believe in and want to support, then make sure you are ready to stand behind it; otherwise your message will fall flat. Value congruence cannot be a one-time thing, based on whatever cause hashtag is trending or news story is gathering attention. It needs to permeate your company and your actions. Good works can sell, but you can't do good works to sell. That's the Pepsi difference.

---

[2] https://backchannel.com/pepsi-would-like-the-world-to-buy-a-coke-fdf928dc3c05

Lesson 62

UnSelling Is the Bombdiggity

BACK IN THE OLD DAYS, when a company did wrong by us there wasn't much we could do. We could write a sternly worded letter or tell our neighbor Ted when he asked about our lawn-care company. We could vent to the other people waiting in line for service or vent to the other wedding guests at our table about the caterer. Now, review sites and other forms of public customer feedback such as Facebook and Twitter have fundamentally disrupted this old order. Today, a single complaint, posted by a person who has little to no past online influence can spread around the world. We make purchase decisions based on the collective opinions of friends, family, and strangers, and we trust them more than any commercial.

Companies have reacted in a number of ways. It's common to see requests for positive reviews at order terminals, receipts, and store fixtures. Follow-up emails now regularly request reviews, complete with links and suggestions. On the shiftier end, we see sites like Fiverr, where reviews can be purchased $5 at a time. When *UnSelling* launched in 2015, we created a mock video testimonial collection[1] (the best money we've ever spent) and sent a script to 14 Fiverr members that read:

> Wow! The new book *UnSelling: The New Customer Experience* is the BOBMDIGITY! I've never read a business book this EPIC! Trust me! Go to UnSellingTheBook.com now! Wooooo!

The book wasn't out yet. None of them had read it. But the reviews rolled in anyway, and they were magnificent. We took them all, and made what may very well be our greatest creation to date.

At the end of our video, we reminded people that not every review is to be trusted, especially not these. Obviously, we created the video in fun and to demonstrate what *UnSelling* would be all about, but the underlying issue around paid, fake reviews is no laughing matter. Reviews like these, even some featuring the same "actors," are used to sell health products. People believing these to be real product users (or worse, medical professionals) make purchases that can negatively affect their well-being, waste their valuable money and time, and even make them sick.

Here are some of the lessons from the making of our fake testimonial video:

1. Some people think fake testimonials aren't a big deal. Most of the feedback we received when we shared the video was lighthearted and pretty dismissive. It came as little surprise to these people that companies buy testimonials on sites like Fiverr, and they felt it really wasn't a big deal. We can't see how a person in a lab coat claiming to be a health care professional and promoting supplements for $5 a pop, *isn't* a big deal.

2. Some people think fake reviews *are* a really big deal. Take the CBC show Marketplace, which sent its wonderful crew out to the *UnPodcast* studio to interview Scott about fake reviews and their danger. It turned out that one of the reviewers they'd been previously investigating was in our video! According to Marketplace, "False or misleading advertising is prohibited by the Competition Act. Any

---

[1] https://www.facebook.com/UnMarketing/videos/10153444963285942/

business, website, or person who makes, buys, or sells fake testimonials could be liable—both the actor providing the testimonial and the company that hires them."[2]

3. We all need to be aware of fake testimonials to make informed choices. Don't trust everything you read online, do your homework, read the labels, and seek reviews from those you trust.

4. Acting as businesses, create products and services worth authentic positive reviews and share those. Take the time you would have spent finding and paying people for phony reviews and focus it on creating experiences that garner real ones.

Our video concluded with a montage of all the reviewers saying the words "trust me" in succession. Twelve people, $60, twelve "trust me"s—and not one of them worth believing. Trust us; you can't believe every review you read.

---

[2] http://www.cbc.ca/news/business/video-review-testimonial-marketplace-1.3953793

Lesson 63

Because the World Needs More Parent Shaming—Get Off Your Phone!

WE LOVE WHEN PEOPLE AND businesses take a stand. One of the best things about the online world is our ability to connect with like-minded people and share issues that matter to us—that's what community is built on. However, as issues bring people together, they can also tear them apart. The Internet didn't invent this, human relationships did.

Few topics unite and divide as much as parenting. From pregnancy to college, it seems everyone has an opinion they're passionate about or judgmental about, depending on which side of the fence they sit. While running her nursing-bra company, Alison constantly found herself walking the brand tightrope, carefully negotiating the conversation around breast-feeding. To get involved or not to get involved—that was the question.

Our answer is: it depends. Consider the issue and how important it is to you; is this the hill you want to plant your flag on? And if so, are you ready to die up on that hill? Remember the capacity for your opinion to spread. Be prepared for absolutely no reaction—or headline news—because both can happen.

When a sign from the door of a daycare center in Hockley, Texas, went viral, the feedback online was heated. The letter read:

> You are picking up your child! GET OFF YOUR PHONE!!!! Your child is happy to see you! Are you happy to see your child?? We have seen children trying to hand their parents their work they completed and the parent is on the phone. We have heard a child say, "Mommy, mommy, mommy . . ." and the parent is paying more attention to their phone than their own child. It is appalling. Get off your phone![1]

We have no doubt that someone well intentioned wrote this letter. Their passion and concern come through in all caps, as does their judgment. The question is whether they meant this message for a few individuals or the world. A strong stand such as this could lose them customers and likely attract new ones of like mind. The lesson here is that what's important isn't the consequences necessarily; it's whether or not they're prepared to live with them. Well-meaning employees might find themselves fired over something like this if it wasn't a stance the larger brand was prepared to take.

---

[1] http://www.self.com/story/viral-day-care-sign

Lesson 64

Freestyle Your Brand

A FEW YEARS AGO WE were in New York City at the Jacob Javits Center for a trade show and wandered up to a local McDonald's to grab a drink. There was this crazy-looking pop machine (soda to our U.S. readers), and it dazzled us with a seemingly endless number of drink choices. The future was here, and there would be strawberry lemonade and diet cherry cola for everyone! The Coke Freestyle machine had captured our hearts.

We had no idea at the time that we were part of a brand research and development experiment—a delicious vanilla root beer–flavored exercise in discovering what customers want. It turned out that Coca-Cola was collecting data from these machines and using the data to decide which drinks people wanted, with the intent of giving us back the most popular ones on store shelves, starting with Cherry Sprite.

According to Consumerist.com, Bobby Oliver (the director of Sprite & Citrus Brands for Coke) said, "The advantage of using Freestyle data is that the data comes from real customers drinking real beverages, not from market research surveys or people ticking a box. There's proven data that people actually love it."[1] In an *Ad Age* interview back in 2014, Jennifer Mann, VP-general manager of Coke Freestyle said, "Freestyle machines have poured more than 5 billion servings and thousands of flavor permutations. A related mobile app that allows people to name and save their favorite combinations and then have Freestyle machines automatically pour them has had more than a million downloads."[2] A million downloads in 2014, 5 billion servings—those are mind-blowing numbers.

Our lesson from Coke could be about the value of using feedback in decision making, even if you're a large, established brand. It could be to look for ways you could be collecting data that you aren't currently utilizing or how digital innovations and tools like apps can make that possible. But for us, the most important branding lesson from Coke is that no matter what the data has shown and no matter how many new products they create and promote, they don't drop the ones that made them who they are. Blackberry Sprite and diet cherry root beer may come and go, but Coke, the cornerstone product upon which the kingdom sits, is forever. Learn from Coke—don't innovate yourself out of what makes you great.

---

[1] https://consumerist.com/2017/02/13/sprite-cherry-now-exists-because-of-the-coke-freestyle-machine/
[2] http://adage.com/article/dataworks/coke-freestyle-dispenses-insights-soft-drinks/295661/

Lesson 65

When Charity Flows

SINCE LAUNCHING THE UNPODCAST, OUT of 200-plus episodes we've had just two live guests, and we've done one Skype interview—not exactly the podcast norm.

We just don't like most people. Not you wonderful reader, all the other people.

On episode 139, "An Unprecedented Episode,"[1] we invited Charity Water founder Scott Harrison to join us via Skype to talk about the organization's history and goals for the future as they celebrated their 10th anniversary. Being fans and past donors, it was a great honor to speak to Scott, and we had a lot of fun learning from him.

Why did we want to speak to Scott Harrison and learn about Charity Water?

1. We love the name Scott.
2. We have been continually impressed by Charity Water.

---

[1] http://www.unmarketing.com/2016/09/07/139-an-unprecedented-episode/

We first learned about Charity Water when one of our friends online shared that she was waiving her fees as a photographer in order to help the cause; she was giving away free headshots in exchange for a donation. One of the best things about social media is learning about new causes, because your friends care about them. This builds immediate trust in the charity, because the trust you have in your connections is immediately carried over to the cause. If the cause means something to our friends, then it means something to us.

Scott started Charity Water after coming out of a job in the nightlife industry. He realized he wanted to do something different:

"I had become the worst person I knew."

He left the vices and opulence of his club-promoter life behind and decided to make a change. He sold everything he owned and dedicated himself to giving back. He joined a humanitarian organization and moved to Liberia, where he witnessed extreme poverty for the first time. The lack of access to clean water he saw shocked him. This represented a complete 180-degree turn from the life he had led before, where $10 water bottles were left unopened in clubs without a second thought. He worked with others who were dedicating their time to helping communities and was inspired especially by one man, Dr. Gary Parker, a plastic surgeon who had planned to volunteer for one year but stayed for 29.[2] Scott spent two years in Liberia learning all he could and returned to New York with a new perspective, wanting to solve the water crisis.

He began by seeking donations from the community he knew—people at nightclubs. Early on, Scott experienced the power of story-telling, finding that he could be a "bridge" connecting the stories he had heard and seen with his own eyes to others who hadn't known about them previously. Scott also believed in sharing real stories—not overly produced or glossed over, but authentic stories—to "move people toward greater compassion."

As he spoke to friends about Charity Water he learned very quickly that there was a big problem—people didn't trust charities; in fact, 42% of Americans don't trust charities. He knew he needed to create a new

---

[2] Ibid.

charitable business model that could challenge these concerns and build trust. He did this by focusing on four steps:

1. *Handling money differently.* He divided finances into two separate accounts—one that funded the work (which would allow 100% of public donations to go directly to people in need) and one for overhead (funded by a separate, smaller group).
2. *Using technology to show impact.* Because none of the public donations were used for overhead, Charity Water could track donations to projects and demonstrate impact more easily. It began putting every water project on Google Earth and Google Maps. Drilling rigs now have Twitter accounts and GPS trackers, all in the name of transparency and sharing results with donors.
3. *Building a beautiful brand.* Scott's goal was to stay away from a "poverty mentality" and to create a brand that looked more like Apple or Nike. Because overhead funding was separate from public, project-oriented funding, Charity Water could accomplish this without taking away from the good work it wanted to accomplish.
4. *Partnering with local organizations and agencies.* From the start, Charity Water would not be sending Westerners to Africa or Asia. It would instead partner with local organizations and fund them so that the work was sustainable.

The goal of Charity Water over the years hasn't changed: to deliver clean water to every human being alive today. In 10 years, it has brought clean water to 6.3 million people, solving 1% of the global water crisis. Going forward, Scott said his team wants to work even faster, focusing on more remote areas where getting water to people is even harder. He hopes to keep elevating the conversation around the water crisis, bringing it into more people's minds, continuing to build the community, and committing more people to subscription giving.

Some of the ideas that wowed us most when speaking with Scott were:

■ Designing a program so that if someone abandoned their donation, Charity Water could email that person and let them know that if they changed their mind, another donor would match their donation.

- The Spring; this was a subscription donation plan for $30 every month, enough to give one person clean water every month.
- After finding that they were losing donors in the subscription programs because credit cards would be lost or expire, Charity Water offered donor matches to those who would switch to an automatic transfer from their bank account.

Both for-profit and nonprofit organizations can learn from Charity Water. It nourishes a growing community by connecting organizations with authentic stories, using technology and innovation. Even with a focus on subscription programs, it loves supporting the grassroots creativity of its donors. For example, one guy recently listened to Nickelback for seven consecutive days and raised $36,000 online. If that's not commitment to a cause, we don't know what is.

Lesson 66

Romantic Atlantic

WE WRITE AND TALK A lot about seeing negative brand attention as an opportunity to be awesome. You can't always avoid being in the spotlight, but you can control how you handle the whole thing. Every interaction with your market is a chance to move the needle for your brand.

On a flight from Los Angeles to New York, Gilbert Ott was injured when a beverage cart came loose after takeoff, rolled down the aisle, and hit him. The cart wasn't latched properly, and because he was wearing an eye mask, Mr. Ott never saw it coming. It smashed into him, completely unexpectedly, and he was badly injured. He tried to contact the airline afterward and sent photos and shared his experience with them. He expected someone at the airline would reach out to him, but instead, "basically three weeks on from the initial event, I was finally was contacted via telephone from customer service (as opposed to liability and risk management team in response to an injury) to be offered a whopping

188

$200 voucher as a final gesture of goodwill, or if I opted, instead 10,000 American AAdvantage miles."[1]

He'd paid about $600 for a one-way ticket for a flight on which he was injured. He was not refunded for the ticket and not promised a refund of any kind. He spent $200 in medical expenses as a result of the injury and was given $200 in travel vouchers for pain and suffering. This is not the same as cash, because the vouchers expire and need to be used on travel—likely not something he's hoping to do anytime soon.

You might think this is a story about American Airlines and how not to treat your customers, but it's not. After his story was posted online it was shared extensively, and the news traveled around the world. Because we're no strangers to travel or complaining about airlines, we learned about Mr. Ott's experience when the story was sent to us multiple times by UnMarketing fans. It seems we weren't the only ones listening. Shortly after sharing his story, Mr. Ott received a surprise in the mail—flowers from Virgin Atlantic.

The flowers came with a note that read, "We might not be who you expected these to be from, but we heard what happened and everyone at Virgin Atlantic wishes you a speedy recovery. And in case you ever fly AA (American) again, we've got you covered. Get Well soon. —The Virgin Atlantic Team."[2] With the flowers, they had sent an entire ground crew kit of elbow and knee pads along with other protective equipment.

Maybe American Airlines should be hiring the Virgin Atlantic team to handle its customer service. The brand lesson from Virgin Atlantic is the value of listening—not only to your own customers, not only to the angry ones or the happy ones—but to your broader market as well. Opportunities present themselves all the time to listen, to empathize, to help, and to have a little fun. We can't find these opportunities without listening.

---

[1] http://www.godsavethepoints.com/news/2016/12/6/my-painful-nightmare-flight-with-american-airlines

[2] http://www.godsavethepoints.com/news/2016/12/10/virgin-atlantic-flowers-card-american-airlines-pr-burn

Photo credit: Gilbert Ott

Lesson 67

More than a Gimmick

IN *UNSELLING*, WE WROTE AN entire chapter about our UnRealtor Petrus Engelbrecht, who won our hearts by leaving a box of donuts from Las Vegas on our doorstep. The moral of the story was that we love donuts and possibly also that Scott will eat things left on our doorstep by strangers. The thing is, the donuts weren't a random gift. Petrus had seen Scott speak and decided he wanted to be on our radar. He did some research—listened to the *UnPodcast*—and learned we love Ronald's Donuts in Las Vegas.

He contacted a colleague in Vegas, had a dozen sent over, and delivered them to our home with a personal note. Then, when it came time for us to buy a home, Petrus was the obvious choice, and we reached out to him. If he hadn't provided wonderful service, we never would have worked with him. But from early on, all the way through the process, Petrus went above and beyond to make our experience buying a home as stress-free as possible. The donuts got our attention, but it was his work that got our business.

When this story crossed our desk back in the fall, we were immediately rooting for Lucas Yla and his sweet way of getting in front of possible future employers.[1] Yla was able to get his résumé in the hands of 10 top advertising agencies and 30 technology companies. Armed with a list of target companies and a box of pastries, he dressed as a courier and delivered free donuts to their offices. Inside the boxes were notes with his contact information and a message: "Most résumés end up in trash. Mine—in your belly."

Photo credit: Lucas Yla

---

[1] http://www.adweek.com/creativity/guy-posed-donut-delivery-man-get-agencies-and-try-land-job-173882/

Yla teaches us an important branding lesson about creativity and determination. When we believe in our product and/or our service, sometimes all we need it an opportunity to get in the front door. We try learning from other's success, we emulate their processes and plans, but sometimes all we need to do is look inward and find a unique way to introduce who we are. Remember, the donuts only got Yla the employers' attention, it didn't get him hired (although we hope he was; if not, call us—we like you). Once you have your market's attention, that is the time to wow them with your business. We spend so much time trying to get attention that sometimes we forget what we're going to do once we get it.

A word of caution: don't let your job-résumé creativity or your business creativity in general be only gimmick deep. A gimmick alone doesn't truly show anyone value. According to Senior VP and Creative Director for Marketing Agency Deutsch Zaid Al-Asady, "If a gimmick takes up more time, like when you have people who send a big package and then you have someone in the mail room who has to walk around the entire agency handing individual things out . . . it can be a little off-putting and it also lacks personality."[2]

Don't make people do extra work to hire you or to get to know you and your brand. Valuing the time of others and creating convenience is a key factor for building loyalty. As Lynn Power, CEO of JWT in New York, said "I personally don't really appreciate the gimmicks. What I do respond to, though, I've had some recent grads that have reached out to me on LinkedIn with a really thoughtful note. Say, 'Hey, I'm looking to get into the business. I'd love to pick your brain for 10 minutes.' Yes, I'll do that. I will respond."[3] A gimmick alone doesn't show care or concern for your audience. Do the work; research and get to know the company you want to work for and then add some creativity as a special touch.

---

[2] http://www.adweek.com/brand-marketing/what-you-can-learn-from-the-crazy-ways-these-job-seekers-got-a-foot-in-the-door/

[3] Ibid.

Lesson 68

Medium-Rare Data

SOMETIMES THE EFFECT OF DISRUPTION on a brand is clear and direct, and we can fall into the trap of overlooking the less obvious ripple effects change can bring. For example, environmental concerns lead to innovations in electric cars, and now we have Tesla. This connection is pretty clear. However, there are a lot of other industries and brands affected by electric car innovations:

- Traditional car and fuel companies may experience decreased market share and may consider innovations of their own.
- Gas stations may see less traffic and consider adding charging stations.
- Customers who seek to add charging stations at home will need emerging businesses to install and maintain them.
- Quieter driving could lead to new challenges in urban planning.
- Service businesses who previously focused on maintaining traditional cars may suffer when upgrades are no longer installed but are uploaded.
- Educational institutions that taught and trained traditional trades and services may suffer and need to adapt to innovations.
- Batteries will need to be disposed of and replaced.

If you're selling chocolate bars in gas stations and your sales start to decrease, would you think to put the blame on Tesla? Maybe you should. If you don't truly understand the complexities of change and how they affect your brand, then you can't find effective solutions.

To further demonstrate, we have a story written by the brilliant Tom Webster. Tom is Vice President at Edison Research, co-author of *The Mobile Commerce Revolution*, and a regular UnMarketing book contributor. He's an expert in market research and analysis and also happens to be one of our favorite people.

They Also Serve, Who Only Stand and Grill (or the Stories We Don't Tell)

Every year, media studies like The Infinite Dial[1] and others report the growing amount of time we spend consuming media of all forms, largely aided by the presence of the always-online supercomputers in our pockets. Of course, *everything* can't go up—we aren't getting more hours in a day. In fact, one of the forms of "media" that has demonstrably declined over the past decade is *physical* word of mouth. As we spend more time with our faces in screens, we are spending less time with our faces in—er—other faces.

The folks at Kingsford Charcoal realized this, because they could see it in their sales. With fewer social gatherings and get-togethers, there were fewer barbecues. Their response was to commission a whole bunch of market research to segment the various customers for grilling products and to determine the motivations and desires of those segments. The result of all this research was to identify a segment they called "Everyday Grillers,"[2] including a deep dive into Hispanic grillers using ethnographic research, shop-alongs, and extensive copy testing to figure out what made the EGs tick and *why* they grilled so much.

Kingsford pivoted its entire strategy not around the product (it's compressed carbon) but around encouraging, fostering, and providing

[1] http://www.edisonresearch.com/infinite-dial-2017/
[2] http://thearf-org-aux-assets.s3.amazonaws.com/downloads/ogilvy/2016/United-We-Grill.pd

resources for social gatherings. Remember when charcoal ads used to talk about how fast the briquettes would light?

The results were tremendous for such a "non-sexy" product. Among their goals was to realize 2% growth in dollar sales. The campaign produced 5% growth. The insights that the brand team generated from all of this research led to a widespread cross-platform media campaign that included social media as well as time- and weather-based messaging. This story was so compelling, in fact, that the Kingsford team won the Gold Prize for Cross-Platform in 2016's ARF David Ogilvy Awards, which celebrate the use of research in advertising.

I tell you this because I know that there are thousands of stories like this and they don't get told. We tell the stories of Elon Musk. We tell the stories of Jeff Bezos. We celebrate the visionaries who ignore the market, listen to their instincts, and go with their gut to achieve success.

Those are great stories, don't get me wrong.

But let's *also* tell the stories of the courageous, passionate brand marketers who *don't* go with their gut, who *don't* ignore the market, and instead seek out the opinions of their target markets and listen to them. We don't tell those stories enough. "Marketer suppresses instincts, commissions market research, follows recommendations, and achieves increased share" isn't exactly otherwise clarify? *The Tipping Point* or *Purple Cow*. And as a result, we'll never know the names of those marketers.

But to me, they also have great stories to tell. I write this in celebration of the humble briquette, because a friend of mine recently asked me to point him to evidence that "people don't tell the truth on surveys." I'm not sure I would say that. There are good questions and terrible questions. There are questions that people can answer honestly and some they can't. And yes, there are questions that people are less honest about than others. Competent people in my profession know that. And still, in the face of bots, social-media misrepresentation, declining response rates, and other perils of the profession, they bravely soldier forth and ask people about charcoal.

So, here's to you, Kingsford team. Make mine medium rare.

The key lesson for us, is this sentence: "Kingsford pivoted their entire strategy not around the product (it's compressed carbon) but around encouraging, fostering, and providing resources for social gatherings." Kingsford took the information and changed direction with their marketing strategy. Without research, without looking into the *why* behind their dropping sales, they could very easily have made incorrect assumptions resulting in ineffective branding. They could have put money into improving their charcoal, changed its shape, redesigned its packaging, adjusted distribution, or—our favorite marketing misdirect—designed a new logo, and all of these wouldn't have been as effective as "encouraging, fostering, and providing resources for social gatherings." This is the lesson of using data to direct change.

Lesson 69

Hack Your Hiring

BACK IN 2016 AN ARTICLE caught our attention about a relatively small tourism brand whose trademark was being infringed upon by one of the largest media companies around. Seemingly to gain traffic to their site, Travel + Leisure had been co-opting the brand identity (name and marketing material style) of Museum Hack, a New York–based company that offers non-traditional tours of museums. We grabbed our UnMarketing capes and checked out the information. Museum Hack's name and style was their biggest asset. They'd worked hard to build and maintain the brand and were understandably upset to see it being copied by anyone, let alone a large media outlet.[1] How Museum Hack handled the trademark infringement is a lesson in itself. If you want to learn more, we discussed it on *UnPodcast*, Episode 129, "Hack The Museum."[2] For *UnBranding*, we've decided to focus on some of the other lessons Museum Hack has taught us.

We learned more about Museum Hack and loved what they were doing—offering private tours of museums with a unique and modern twist.

---

[1] https://museumhack.com/travel-leisure/

[2] http://www.unmarketing.com/tag/hack-the-museum/

On a trip to New York City, Alison booked a tour with them for herself and Benjamin (age 13) and it was *awesome*! The tour guide was engaging and entertaining, customizing the tour to Ben's interests. Ben loved it so much that he and Alison ended up spending the rest of the afternoon at the museum after the tour ended, and they even returned the next day for more.

Museum Hack offers private and public tours of museums, for everyone from a pair of Canadians like us, to bachelorette parties and team-building events. They also provide consulting services to museums, training staff on engagement and storytelling. Their director of marketing, Michael Alexis, told us in an interview that although their core customer is millenials, the age groups they see are growing and changing all the time, the corporate groups being especially diverse. They have mostly informal relationships with the museums they tour, although this is moving toward becoming more formal.

As brands we are all trying to attract new customers and build our community, so what can we learn from Museum Hack? It is the brand value of good hiring. Most tour guides come from performance backgrounds— people comfortable in front of an audience. Tours are customized, and guides need to be able to adapt and plan on the fly. This requires both a knowledge of art and art history and an understanding of each museum and its story. Guides need to read their audience, listen to tour members, answer questions, and make the experience fun and engaging, leaving customers with an emotional experience. The hiring process is more akin to auditioning than the standard job interview, with an important part of the process including candidates giving a practice museum tour that focuses on three key objects in the museum. The CEO has said that it's "harder to get into Museum Hack than to get into Harvard." The work force is entirely remote, with support staff, marketing, and sales working from home and at cafés with occasional co-working.

It's easy to see why hiring of this quality has lead to such an innovative business. Museum Hack has also begun focusing more on consulting with companies. Bloomingdale's in New York hired them to hack their flagship store, creating an in-store scavenger hunt where employees looked at the history of the store and completed challenges based on objects in the space.

A major sports retailer hired them recently to teach storytelling to their staff and look at the brand history, so they can share this with customers. We also love their social-media marketing (a rarely said statement by us), where they share pieces of art with a special Museum Hack twist, like our personal favorite shown here.

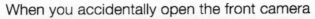
When you accidentally open the front camera

Photo credit: Museum Hack

The term "hack" has never been our favorite word, but we've made an exception for this innovative company. As demonstrated in their corporate training manifesto, "Everyone can make their best contribution. The best companies aren't about a few superstars that carry the team; it's about everyone being empowered and driven to make their best contribution. This equality applies to everyone from the front-line workers to the executive group. No exceptions." Museum Hack truly exemplifies this idea in their own hiring and passes that along to their guests and clients.

Lesson 70

Kind, True, Helpful, and Refreshing

BEER BRAND CORONA RECENTLY GOT some press about the generosity of its founder that turned out not to be true. Several media outlets in the UK falsely reported that the late CEO of the Corona brewery Grupo Modelo, Antonino Fernandez, had left about 200 million pounds to the residents of the small village where he was born and raised.[1] While Mr. Fernandez was a generous man who gave much to his hometown, including financing renovations and road work and providing citizens with clean water, he did not in fact leave this large sum to the town in his will.

Media outlets who shared the false story all had to go back and write retractions and updates, but what about all the people who posted it on their Facebook pages and other platforms? Surely, the formal outlets should have fact-checked the story before printing, but we feel the same should be true for each of us. Today, news can spread in an instant and this is a huge responsibility; in fact it's our biggest responsibility as online citizens in the age of disruption. Everyone is in a mad rush to be first to share, because

---

[1] http://metro.co.uk/2016/11/25/so-coronas-founder-isnt-making-everyone-a-millionaire-after-all-6282851/#ixzz4UkfRqcbF

being first also means you become the source, driving traffic and attention to you. We beg of you to avoid this trap. Don't focus on being first—focus on being right, first.

While the Corona story seems pretty harmless (unless, we suppose, you were a resident who bought a house on the basis of the false promise), some stories can have far-reaching, damaging results. We love the capacity for our online world to promote change and consumer advocacy, but sharing a fake story about a business can lead to them losing their livelihoods. Once the story is out there, it is exponentially harder to correct it. You just can't put the toothpaste back in the tube.

Don't assume this is only the responsibility of large outlets or even of people with large followings; any one person, with even one follower, has the ability today to change a company's brand. Social media is an amplification tool, and it amplifies indiscriminately. Before you share, ask yourself three questions:

1. Is it kind?
2. Is it true?
3. Is it helpful?

Now, if you're an UnMarketing fan (which we assume you are, seeing as you're reading this), you may find these rules a bit funny coming from us. We regularly share stories about company screw-ups. We have an entire half of a book titled *The Book of Business UnAwesome*, for goodness, sake. But we always, always, always ask these three questions before posting anything. And if you take one lesson to heart from all of these, we hope it's this one.

Lesson 71

Ghost Restaurant

Your brand isn't what you say it is. It isn't a carefully crafted press release or advertising campaign. Your brand is what your customers or would-be market think of when they think of you. It's dynamic and evolves with each brand interaction. What matters in branding isn't in your hands, it's in your customers' hands.

When you think of a restaurant, a few things may come to mind: the menu, prices, proximity to other destinations, take-out options, and even the political views of its CEO. Most of the time, when you think of a restaurant, you think of a place. Factors such as comfort, cleanliness, customer service, and how casual or fancy the dining is would all affect your choices. Even when you order their food for home, these physical factors affect your choice, because they're all part of the brand experience.

So what happens when some restaurants offering delivery aren't actually physical locations at all?[1] They have kitchens, of course (this

---

[1] https://consumerist.com/2017/01/20/ghost-restaurants-with-no-tables-thrive-on-delivery-apps/

isn't the Starship *Enterprise* just yet), but they don't have locations where you can eat in; these are delivery only. From a branding perspective, this creates a few issues. It's not a very common occurrence, so customers mostly aren't expecting food from a delivery kitchen that isn't a restaurant. Some people may order take-out only from places they've actually eaten in, and that might present an issue.

For some of us (Alison included), seeing a physical restaurant allows a certain amount of transparency. When she can see how clean the restaurant is, that gives her an idea about how clean the kitchen is, and cleanliness in food preparation is kind of important to her. And finally, if there's an assumption that restaurants have physical locations, then using this assumption without providing the true information is dishonest, and like cleanliness, trust in food preparation is also really important.

With digital innovations making online ordering the norm for delivery (we can't remember the last time we called to order pizza), sites like Seamless and Eat24 have become popular by offering a collection of options for ordering, like the virtual version of the old-time phone books. While users love being able to order everything from burgers to sushi all in one spot, sometimes they don't realize they aren't ordering from brick-and-mortar restaurants. For example, the Green Summit Group operates several food-delivery services out of central locations in New York and Chicago and acts as a collection of "restaurants" online.

We understand the appeal as business owners. Other than food and supplies, location is a top expense when starting a restaurant, especially in an urban center like New York. Without needing to rent, operate, and care for a physical space, costs go down and opportunities increase for those looking to enter the market. Green Summits cofounder Peter Schatzberg says they allow people to "operate a viable restaurant business with a minimal footprint."[2]

The lesson from our restaurantless restaurants is this: innovation can create exciting opportunities, but ensuring that your market is ready for

---

[2] https://www.fastcompany.com/3064075/fast-cities/hold-the-storefront-how-delivery-only-ghost-restaurants-are-changing-take-out

these innovations is key to your success. It's up to companies like Green Summit to make sure customers know where they're ordering from and that standards are on par with brick-and-mortar locations. Sharing the benefits of this type of food-service business with others has to be their second full-time job. If you innovate and your market feels tricked or simply isn't ready to accept the change, you will hurt your brand and leave customers feeling cheated.

Lesson 72

Sort-of-Okay Western

FEW INDUSTRIES DEMONSTRATE THE DICHOTOMY within the age of disruption better than hospitality. Think about how you chose the last hotel you stayed in. Maybe you saw a photo of it on Instagram or Facebook shared by one of your trusted friends and decided to check out the site. You might have received an email promotion from that time you stayed in one of their other locations and took advantage of the discount. Perhaps one of the characters on your latest Netflix bender stayed there, and it caught your attention. Or maybe that's where your conference is, and like us you just don't want to have to walk too far to the opening breakfast. It's possible you aren't staying in a hotel at all but rather in an Airbnb that you chose from a collection of searchable options and detailed reviews. How we choose in hospitality is continually evolving, and this is how digital innovation has disrupted the industry.

Now, in each of these cases, you still end up consuming the same type of product, and what you want from that product hasn't changed in the least. Every option will be judged on the same loyalty factors—comfort, convenience, cost, and congruency. If you get a good sleep, are treated well, and find the space clean and inviting, and the hotel adds to your overall traveling experience, you will leave a happy customer. No innovation around finding the hotel will ever change what makes the stay great. No one ever said, "The front desk staff were rude, the bathroom was dirty, and I had to walk a mile to my meeting—but did you see how easy it was to find the Hotel Craptastic online?! Let's go back next month!"

Start with a good product, innovate second. The experiences of your current customers are what drive the content of the digital conversation. Too many of us are stuck battling the negative reviews rather than fixing the negative experience. When your hotel draws negative feedback, there are a few things you can do. You can reply graciously and make changes to your location accordingly. You can ignore the comment(s) publically, while still making changes internally. Or you can simply continue to provide the same terrible service, while working on your new Snapchat campaign. Because millennials, right?!

This brings us to the Best Western chain—or as we've been calling them, the We're Sort-of Trying Western—which opted to ignore any of the previously mentioned options and decided to reply publically, defensively, and rudely, all while blaming the Internet for letting people speak and throwing their staff under the bus. Check out one manager's reply to an upset customer on TripAdvisor:

Dear James G.: Thank you for your stay with us. I do apologize for your disappointing stay with us. I have noted your comments and will review them with our staff members to make improvements. Unfortunately, mistakes can happen with our staff as our hotel is working with a mostly Native population that have not had privileged education available in most parts of the country. The hotel does our best to train them to improve their quality of life. We hope our guests from outside the reservation can also introduce kindness to them as they are very nice people learning to service a more sophisticated and well-traveled public. Thank you.

When news spread about the racist manager who had not only commented this way but also fired the staff member in question, Best Western released the following statement:

> Best Western values diversity and the fair treatment of all individuals. We are committed to ensuring guests have an exemplary experience at each of our independently owned and operated hotels. Having spoken to the hotel's leadership, we have been assured that the comments were never intended to be offensive or demeaning, and that they truly regret that they can be misconstrued. The hotel truly appreciates being a valued member of its community.[1]

We see nothing "misconstrued" about any of this. The manager replied to a bad review with the intent of blaming staff he considered to be less than valuable. He showed his true colors and made the company look bad along with his staff and what we assume are thousands of other good staff members at this and other locations. He was branding. We suppose our lesson here could be how not to apologize, but instead let's focus on communication.

Clearly there was a problem at this location between staff and management, and it took an incident like this one for people to notice. Companies need active and engaged HR departments to guide practice, communicate with workers, and watch over interactions between staff and management. Best Western needs an active HR department so it can fire managers like this one and make room for someone new who truly can appreciate and work with other staff members and create customer experiences deserving of the name Best.

[1] http://www.12news.com/mb/news/local/arizona/best-western-under-fire-for-offensive-social-media-post/299957730

Lesson 73

There Is No Urgency in Mediocrity

IT'S NO SECRET THAT WE love Las Vegas. Together we've been there over 100 times—not bad for a couple from Canada! From hotels, to restaurants, to retailers, our love for frequent trips means we've also been on dozens of email lists from Vegas businesses. Some we subscribed to for news and updates, some for sales and new products, and some just to see how they were using email—you know, since we write and speak about that kind of stuff. We unsubscribed from most of them pretty quickly. Some lost us because their frequency of communication far outweighed our interest or their ability to create good content. Others just got lost inside our noisy inboxes until they became irrelevant.

And then there is the one that broke Scott's email heart. It's rare to have a current, ecstatic customer unsubscribe from your newsletter—the kind of customer who wants to keep giving you their money and regularly does just that happily. But that is just what happened to Scott, when he had to end his email relationship with Caesars Palace.

It all started with the following subject line.

From: Total Rewards Las Vegas ＞   Hide

To: Scott Stratten ＞

Very Important! This Is Really Urgent: See Your Amazing January Offer Now
Today at 6:08 PM

Picture the panic in Scott's eyes. "What's wrong, happiest place on earth? What can I do to help?"

If you saw this subject line what would you think it was about? If it was from an unknown sender, something in your spam folder, you'd ignore it. But this came from a known, trusted brand, one we spend a lot of money and time with. Scott clicked it right away, ready to make a donation or give of his time—whatever they needed. He was expecting something really urgent, like a disaster or a free trip for two for a week, during which we'd meet Elton John and sing with Celine Dion!

The offer was for $10.

If we booked our flights from Toronto to Las Vegas and a three-night stay at the hotel *immediately*, we'd get $10 in "free" slot play. Just think of it! After spending thousands of dollars, we'd have a little extra. We could use a slot machine—once!

That was the end for Scott. He unsubscribed. The fake urgency was the icing on the over-priced, Vegas Strip cake.

He had stayed through boring emails without much to say. He'd even stayed when bombarded with emails from every casino in their chain. He visited one in Philadelphia once, and bam—weekly emails from Mississippi, New Orleans, Vegas, and Atlantic City. You couldn't switch preferences or reduce frequency. He stayed through non-stop terrible offers for insultingly little compared with the money we'd spent as customers. Offering a loyal, high-value customer the same or less than a brand-new customer is a sure-fire way to introduce brand competition. (Also see: cable companies, banks, and cell phone providers.)

Casinos are the godfathers of loyalty-points cards for pioneering data collection on customers. As Diamond members at Caesars for the fifth year in a row, we've provided the casino with all the information they need to communicate with us effectively. They know where we stay, eat, and shop and the frequency with which we do so. They should know us better than we know ourselves. They should have known enough to send us emails with a 100% open rate without needing to resort to lazy, all-caps, fake-urgent subject lines.

We haven't changed our mind about staying at Caesars, but we have shut down the communication, which left us open to offers from competing properties. A wink and a compliment from the Cosmopolitan and we spent three days there. Our money decided not to come back with us, so they kept that too.

Our branding lesson from Caesars is that much of the time, our competitors' opportunities are our fault. We treat current customers like someone we've been married to for 40 years, when the last 35 haven't been that great. We overwhelm with email frequency, send lackluster offers that pale in comparison to the ones we use for new-customer acquisition, and ignore the information they've already given us in good faith. Don't be the brand that cries urgent; when you really want to reach your customers, they won't be listening.

Lesson 74

Are You a Seeder or a Leecher?

To us and many others, BitTorrent is synonymous with Napster and illegal downloads and with burning CDs on 2xburner, only to have another one mess up after two days of waiting for it to finish. The world is classified into seeders and leechers—those who would give and those who would take.

You might say, BitTorrent has a bit of a brand image problem when it comes to encouraging advertisers to use their platform—a brand image problem they're working to fix by getting the word out that they aren't a piracy platform but just a tool that can be used that way—the way a coat hanger is meant for hanging clothes, not breaking into cars.

Today BitTorrent is used by labels to legally release music, by broadcasters to legally distribute their shows, and the UK government to keep its citizens informed on where their tax money is being spent. With 170 million active monthly users (63% of whom are under 34), BitTorrent now markets itself as a "way for artists to sell their work without selling their souls" and "the Internet's own record store."

"The company recently brokered a deal with General Electric for a new campaign where a song created by Matthew Dear out of sounds from GE

machines like subsea compressors and jet engines could be downloaded via the company's Bundle. Since the launch on Aug. 27, 1.5 million people have downloaded the content. Just 30,000 people streamed it on Sound-Cloud, where the song was also hosted."[1]

Our lesson from BitTorrent is that brands exist in the eyes of their consumers. If you want to change their perception, you need to make it your mission to share who you are with the world. This is true whether you're brand new and building, keeping your brand strong, or rebranding.

---

[1] http://digiday.com/marketing/pitch-deck-bittorrent-shops-advertisers-publishers/

Lesson 75

Peyton's Pizza Palace

WE LOVE FOOTBALL. OUR BASEMENT was set up especially for enjoyment of the NFL superfan package, with giant TV and custom-made reclining seats. We pretend the space is for the kids to watch movies, but they all know it's really for us on Sundays from September to February.

One of the things about watching football from Canada is that we see all the American commercials, many from companies we don't have around here and medications we don't need (yet). Papa John's Pizza is one of these. It's our second favorite Peyton Manning commercial after the DirecTV's NFL Sunday Ticket—the one where he made us want more football and some tapenade to go with it. Alison is a huge Peyton Manning commercial fan.

We've never actually tried Papa John's Pizza; they aren't even a regular option for us. But you don't need to be a customer to have a feeling about a brand. To us, the brand was about football, hanging out with friends, and

Peyton. That was until one of our UnMarketing Facebook fans, Lacy Philips, had this to share about Papa John's CEO:

> My sister's first job was in the kitchen, then she worked in pizza delivery, then she was promoted to a shift manager. We were loyal customers even after she'd moved on to work elsewhere, but their CEO's horrible record with being involved with politics and his company's treatment of their labor force has turned me off of the brand. Every time I see his smug, overly botoxed face on the TV with Peyton Manning, I cringe. Papa John's CEO John Schnautter has inserted himself into the company's ads as a personality for no other reason that I can think of than pure vanity. He's a stiff actor and doesn't add any entertainment value to the myriad TV spots he casts himself in. He is very, very, very rich and yet gives nothing to his local community in Louisville, KY, and annoys his neighbors by building a helipad on his property so he can take a chopper to work on a whim. Contrast that with Peyton Manning, who has a whole children's hospital named after him and regularly donates large sums to charitable causes. The Papa John's product is still my favorite tasting national chain delivery pizza, but I don't order from them anymore and haven't for years based simply on the fact that I disagree with their CEO's politics and think he's the embodiment of the word snob.

Even if someone loves your product, your politics and public persona can make them walk away. We're big fans of this kind of decision making; the best way to change the way companies behave is with your dollars. Our lesson here is to make sure you're asking why when making decisions about who should be the face of your company. We aren't sure if vanity is the reason behind using your CEO, but it sure can look that way. And if you are looking to hire a brand spokesperson, always go with Peyton. You can't beat Peyton.

Lesson 76

The Cadillac of Coffee Shops

THE QUESTION WHY? HAS GOTTEN a really bad rap and is too often dismissed with a "Why not?" We leave this question unanswered far too often in branding.

We need a Snapchat campaign.

We have to start using virtual reality in our marketing.

We should open three new locations.

We can't hire more customer service representatives.

We shouldn't start our own business.

Why?

Please consider why, we beg you. If the answer is any variation of "Because we want to appear cutting edge" with no further reasoning, stop what you're doing—immediately. We won't even send you a bill.

We should open a branded coffee shop.

Why, General Motors, why?

GM opened a Cadillac-branded coffee house in Manhattan. In an attempt to reach a younger crowd, the space features art, retail, and of course coffee. While we love the idea of cool spaces in one of our favorite cities, we have to question whether it would have been wiser to spend the money conducting research on what potential customers are looking for in a car or improving current products and service. The cool-space focus seems to make a lot of assumptions about millennials and the reasons behind their aversion to the classic brand.

As the brilliant Consumerist Community Editor wrote when he shared the story, "Personally, I'm holding out for a Starbucks-branded car."[1] Now that's a product we could get behind.

---

[1] https://consumerist.com/2016/05/13/cadillac-wants-to-attract-millennials-somehow-opens-a-coffee-shop/?utm_source=facebook&utm_medium=socialflow

Lesson 77

Peloton, Fitness, and Creating Motivation

ONE OF ALISON'S FAVORITE CHILDHOOD memories is watching her older sister Jody do the Jane Fonda workout tape in her basement. The ability for a busy parent, working full-time, to simply pop in the VHS tape and turn her house into a gym seemed like the pinnacle of cutting-edge technology. Jane, in all her legwarmer glory, flanked by a crew of energetic women, appeared right in front of you. The future was trim, affordable, and fun, and it was here, in the basement.

The fitness industry is prolific. Our digital age has made it impossible to escape from it. From the latest in workout trends, foods and supplements, fashion and beauty, to product companies such as car manufacturers and travel, fitness is everywhere. I'm not even sure that Jane imagined she'd pioneer a world where Instagram celebrities could deliver entire diet and exercise plans to our phones, or where car companies would feature fit couples with mountain bikes and surfboards hopping from spot to spot with ease.

Along with innovation has come a lot of blaming and shaming. In the past, you needed to compare yourself only to people you met in real life.

Now we are bombarded by images of celebrities with million-dollar bodies, funded in part by our purchases of their health products and promises. It seems everyone has the secret for fitness, all at one low price. Now while the method of delivery may have changed from our basement VHS days, exercise hasn't. Until we can tone up virtually, sweat is still sweat, and we all still actually have to move our bodies for exercise. Innovations have come, but whether it's Richard Simmons on tape or Kayla Itsinis on Instagram, the goal is the same: make people care about movement and then make them actually move.

When we were in Nashville in April for Emma's conference "Marketing United," we had the great pleasure of having dinner with some fine people from Kellogg's. Aside from chatting about marketing and enjoying some of the finest barbeque around, they told us about a cool innovation in fitness that they were clearly obsessed with—the Peloton Cycle. Not only was this top-of-the-line home-exercise bike a favorite because of its quality and small footprint in their homes, they couldn't stop talking about the streaming classes it offered and its online social community. They could access thousands of classes with a variety of difficulties, and they could stream live classes daily (the site says there are 14 live classes per day) and chat with other cyclists using the system. Access to professional teachers, along with the social interaction of the online class and cool features like the ability to cycle through locations around the world made Peloton Cycle's today's Jane Fonda workout.

We asked our UnMarketing Facebook fans for some of their brand stories about fitness. Here are two of our favorites.

Becky Johns wrote,

CrossFit. I thought it was a cult-like obsession that was not any more productive than any other form of exercise. But then after seeing more and more of my friends get into it, I gave it a try. I now love the training style, understand that it's a great program to help individuals progress in their fitness, and that there is really a supportive community aspect. It's a brand I now closely associate with and am proud to call myself a CrossFit athlete.

Pam Ross shared,

Goodlife. I was a member for more than 20 years (of companies they acquired before Goodlife too) and then when I moved to Oakville and asked to transfer gyms, they told me my membership fee would go up to 4 times what I had been paying for 20 years. I called them several times and after long waits on hold, finally spoke to someone who wouldn't help me. Tweeted them and got a very nice public response asking me to DM, never heard a peep from them via DM. Good news was another gym reached out via Twitter and offered a tour and free month. I'm now a member there. I was so frustrated with them that I wrote a blog about it.

In both of these stories, we see how a brand can change with personal interaction. Becky went from being a non-customer with a preconceived notion to being a proud customer because of a positive experience once she tried CrossFit. This seems to be a common experience with the brand. A lesson here for us may be that when customer stories are extremely positive, or as she describes, "cult-like" that non-customers may be intimidated or put off. For Pam, the story is the opposite. Here we have a loyal customer treated badly, which opens her up to the competition. It's smart for the competitor to offer up some free services, to let people try out their gym and make the switch.

Few industries rely more on creating habit than the fitness industry. There isn't a program in the world that will have results without creating habit, making it not only a good business goal but a good goal for customers in general. Innovations like the ones Peloton Cycle are using create a community of motivation—motivation that can help you keep your home gym from becoming a very-expensive-place-to-hang-your-clothes laundry rack.

Our lesson here is to think about how you're creating opportunities for motivation among your customers and would-be market. The tools our disruptive time offer can help to bring people together around the need your product or service solves, and feed your funnel. Motivation is a full-time job. Study your current customers' motivations and learn from them. What brought them in in the first place? What do they love about your company? What would they change?

Lesson 78

Opening Up the Brand Crate

EVEN IN THE STEADIEST OF economic times and even for those with business educations and experience, starting a company can be a scary thing. That first step—whether it is a domain registration, a sketch on a napkin, a late-night conversation with a partner, or a well-thought-out business plan—requires momentum, confidence, trust, and sometimes just not knowing any better.

When Gordon Segal, who founded the company Crate and Barrel with his wife when he was 23 years old, was asked what gave them the confidence to get started so young he said, "The value of being very young is you have all the energy and passion and none of the wisdom."[1]

Wisdom brings an understanding of risk. Whether it involves risking the judgment of others, fear of failure, or financial risk, risk brings doubt, and doubt tends to stop us in our tracks. When we factor in the doubts within ourselves along with those we feel when surrounded by change and innovation, it can be enough to leave those napkins at home. Wisdom also

[1] http://www.npr.org/podcasts/510313/how-i-built-this

221

brings an appreciation for hard work and just how much tenacity and dedication you will need to have to get started and keep going.

Some of our brands were started by serial entrepreneurs who possess a set of skills and attributes that carry their companies forward independent of product. Some, like Mr. Segal, credit blissful ignorance—simply not knowing that they should have been worried about starting at all. Some founders are driven by passion for a certain product or for meeting the needs of a certain community; they may have doubts, but those doubts are outweighed by potential rewards. And like us, some entrepreneurs are simply unemployable control freaks who would rather work around the clock for themselves than 9 to 5 for someone else.

If all the brand stories we've studied have taught us anything, it's that there's no secret formula or perfect time to start a business. Our lesson is that the secret to starting a business in the age of disruption is the same as it's always been: you just need to roll up your sleeves and get to work.

Lesson 79

Time Will Tell

PRINT MEDIA HAS BEEN HIT hard by digital change, or at least that's what digital media is telling us. Today, counting on tomorrow morning's paper for the latest information seems archaic. We watch stories develop in real time online. While this meets our thirst for up-to-the-minute reporting, it also comes with the danger that misinformation will spread like wildfire. Many news outlets have embraced the digital format, offering paid subscriptions and sharing their stories across social-media platforms.

Less news-focused outlets, such as those dedicated to fashion, entertainment, or consumer products have followed suit, welcoming digital media as an opportunity to expand their offerings. As we learned from Haley Overland in our chapter about *Chatelaine*, a content-first focus can allow for the value of a campaign that includes written articles, images, video, and social media.

Time, Inc., a true print powerhouse that includes *Time*, *Sports Illustrated*, and *People* magazine, hasn't been immune to the digital-media disruption. The result has been the company shifting its advertising sales from ads based on title to ads based on category. The reorganization included categories such as "automotive, pharmaceutical and technology/ telecommunications. It was later extended to several others including food and beverage, beauty and retail." The title of each magazine was eventually completely removed from the sales material.[1]

As with any big change, the shift has not been without challenges. The magazines themselves are iconic brands, and many salespeople needed to be convinced of the value of being an "automotive person" rather than a "*Sports Illustrated* person." Time's answer has been in education—making sure customers understand why they've made the change and demonstrating the value of reaching eyes based on content rather than by attaching a product or service to a particular media outlet.

We suppose only time will tell whether they're on the right track. It seems a bit backward to us to dismantle brands decades in the making, in the name of using a digital model to keep print media afloat. Each of those magazines is a unique voice with a unique audience, and blurring the lines may end up eroding the value they bring to the advertising table. Whether or not you agree with the change, the lesson here is about the education focus. To survive disruption we need to adapt, but change is never easy. We need to convince ourselves it's necessary, we need to get our employees on board, and then we need to educate our customers. We can't allow our own assumptions to get in the way. Any reasoning that begins with "well, everyone knows that . . ." can be a dangerous fallacy. Communication is the bridge for all change.

During our research, we had the pleasure of speaking with a senior executive from a major publishing house. The executive and the publisher's PR department wished to remain anonymous, but we can tell you they all have decades of experience in magazine advertising with a number of iconic brands, through periods of tremendous innovation and disruption. For the sake of this lesson, let's call them Dr. Media. They believed the Time, Inc., change that took the iconic magazine brands off the advertising table was unnecessary and could be damaging in the end to the company. They told us it was basically a practice to make print

[1] https://digiday.com/media/compete-time-inc-gets-rid-publishers-category-based-sales-transition-bumpy/

look and feel more digital while ignoring the very things that made the print space valuable.

Dr. Media and the magazine company they are employed by work with some of the most recognizable brands in the world, including Apple, *Covergirl*, and pretty much every car company around, and have adapted to digital innovation. They shared with us that one of the biggest challenges to print media is how digital has created an expectation of free content, while most magazines generate revenue through paying customers. Even so, their magazine audience has remained relatively stable. Much of the credit for this lies in their focus on the consumer while keeping quality at the heart of editorial and brand-sponsored content.

According to Dr. Media, the most dramatic shift during the past few years on the advertising side has been in how advertising and sponsored editorials are created. In the past, a brand would come to the magazine with a budget, and it would be divided among print, digital, and TV. Now the marketing team will reach out to advertisers and create content for them— a proactive conversation that has brought the marketing team front and center as a content creator. This shift has led to better results for brands and generally higher-quality content for the magazine.

If you're a brand looking to work with magazines, Dr. Media's lesson is to focus on who your audience is. The clearer your brief and the better your understanding is of who you're trying to reach, the better your results can be. The Dr. loves how brands are crossing over between traditionally defined areas—for example, beauty products looking at food audiences, automotive brands working with the fitness industry—to create unexpected advertising to delight. He suggests you recognize that people don't fall into individual buckets, and that you work with magazines to find creative ways to cross over.

On the media side, if you're looking to work in print media, Dr. Media wants you to learn that flexibility is the key. You can't think "channel." You may start out working for a TV station, but when the station pivots toward a digital strategy, you need to be ready to make that shift. Everything goes back to the consumer; if you're going to work in media today, you need to know who your reader is.

Lesson 80

Razer's Edge

WE WEREN'T SURE WHETHER WE'D include this one in *UnBranding* or not. We'd love to think that in 2017, or whenever in the future you're reading this (do we have flying cars yet?), common sense would guide you to never, ever do something like this. But the truth is (and one of the main reasons that we're in business) that common sense isn't so common. In the name of being funny, brands make terrible choices every day. Do funny posts and ads get more shares online? Certainly. But forcing the funny, often to the side of causing offense as we see next from Razer, will get you the kind of shares you don't want.

When promoting their new laptop, which featured an SD slot, the company tweeted the following:

RAZER ✓
@Razer

     Follow

You call yourself Pro? S my D.

RETWEETS	LIKES
263	767

10:05 AM - 1 Nov 2016

↩   ↻ 263   ♥ 767   •••

The offensive reference was completely and totally unnecessary, all in the name of seeming edgy and "funny." After a ton of negative feedback, mainly pointing to the fact that sexism in the tech industry and gaming is prolific and no laughing matter, the company deleted the tweet and made the following apology, "We apologize for the SD reader joke. To those who were offended, it was intended as a light-hearted turn of phrase that missed the mark."[1]

There is such a thing as bad press. The apology took its own share of heat from those who felt the tweet was no big deal and called foul, blamed political correctness, and basically said that those offended just "couldn't take a joke." What bothers us most about this, and the main lesson here, is that Razer didn't need to use the attempt at humor to sell their product. The SD card was a feature lacking in other products, most namely Apple laptops, and focusing on its value could have been done in a much more effective way, one that would keep the focus on the product, rather than being offensive.

---

[1] http://gizmodo.com/here-is-a-very-bad-tweet-by-razer-1788451299

Humor is great. We love humor. But as this story indicates, the *why* for using it needs to come first for any brand heading down the funny road. This may also demonstrate that Razer missed the mark in understanding congruence with its market. There may have been a day when a mostly male customer base with a teenager's sense of humor would have loved, or at least ignored, the tweet. But clearly, now was not that day.

Lesson 81

No, We Can't Get You Tickets to *Hamilton*

IN *UNSELLING* WE SPENT SOME time looking at how the music business has changed. Few industries have faced the kind of disruption that musicians, producers, and record companies have had to face. On the delivery side we've seen records and tapes turn into CDs and MP3s and later into streaming services. Digital recordings have been the focus of legal battles, pitting creators against distributors and distributors against the Internet.

On the creation side, as we've seen with photography, technology has put the tools once reserved for professionals into anyone's hands. Our 15-year-old spends his weekends making music and sharing it online seamlessly. We now discover musicians as YouTube sensations, SoundCloud superstars, and social-media pros as platforms that once were an added bonus for celebrities are now a must.

The favorite music innovation in our house is Spotify, a digital music streaming service that offers both a free (with some advertising) option and a premium service that can be access across all devices. Alison uses it every day to create a three-song morning playlist for Tessa, and our ability to download playlists so we can listen without streaming saves us gazillions of dollars (give or take) in data every month.

So you might expect such an innovative platform to focus solely on Snapchat for marketing (or wherever the cool kids are hanging out online these days), but our favorite story about Spotify this year came from some billboards. For you younger readers, a billboard is a huge sign out in the real world where companies would put large words and images for people to see when driving by.

But how did they measure their effectiveness without click rates, you may ask. Heck if we know.

This past year, Spotify decided to use their vast amount of listener data in a billboard campaign where they showed some of the more "bizarre user habits it noticed throughout 2016."[1] Some of the messaging included things like:

- "Dear person who played 'Sorry' 42 times on Valentine's Day, what did you do?"
- "Dear person in the Theater District who listened to the *Hamilton* soundtrack 5,376 times this year, can you get us tickets?"
- "Dear 3,749 people who streamed 'It's the End of the World as We Know It' the day of the Brexit vote, hang in there."

So great, right? We absolutely love the creativity and style, which is perfect for the brand. Sidenote: we may have been the account who listened to the *Hamilton* soundtrack 5,376 times. The lesson here is that old-school marketing tools—such as billboards, magazine ads, and even television commercials—are often ignored in favor of social media, as we jump around to whatever is newest and shiniest. A billboard is just a tool. It isn't inherently poor for marketing a modern company like Spotify. A weak Snapchat campaign is as useless as a bad ad on a bus bench.

---

[1] http://www.adweek.com/creativity/spotify-crunches-user-data-fun-ways-new-global-outdoor-ad-campaign-174826/

Lesson 82

For the Love
of Animals and
the Hatred of
Animal Hair

A LACK OF CONGRUENCE WITH your market's values can drive away custom-ers. While many will put a higher importance on cost or convenience, there will always be those who make ethically motivated purchases. This is especially important if you are a brand that uses congruence in your marketing. Our "healthy" drink companies that weren't so healthy learned this the hard way, as described in Lesson 39, "The Emperor Has No Juice."

Here are two stories about congruence from our UnMarketing Facebook fans.

Janice Quirt wrote,

I used to love Dove and St. Ives. Then I realized that they both test on animals. It was particularly tough with St. Ives as they were known to be cruelty-free and then they were bought by Unilever and can no longer claim that they don't test on animals. Many people just assume that both brands are ok.

Hilary Karnatz wrote,

Bissell. Didn't really like my vacuum. I bought a Shark that I love, but we recently adopted a dog on empty the shelter day (an event held by Bissell). I met Kathy Bissell and she seems so in love with animals and her company. Made me love her company too. My next vacuum will be a Bissell. I will give it another try.

A love of animals coupled with a desire not to harm them is a strong motivator for many people. Some shape their entire lifestyle around this value, choosing cruelty-free products or a vegan diet. They vote with their dollars, steering clear of products tested on animals or any that use animal products. If your company's values align with a cruelty-free market, let people know.

We especially love Hilary Karnatz's story. Not only because we are also animal lovers, support our local animal shelter, and battle dog and cat fur daily in our home, but because the story perfectly demonstrates Bissell's understanding of their market. Who needs a great vacuum? People with pets, that's who. And since we also love pets, why not help to build community around the issue of pet welfare. Bissell helps out some animals, animals get good homes, homes get good animals, and if some of them associate this with the brand—everyone wins. Our lesson here is to think about what connects your customers beyond using your product. It is these connections that truly build community.

Lesson 83

That Week We Sold Socks

When fans started asking to buy *UnPodcast* socks, we needed a solution. We were not set up to sell anything online, and we wanted a platform that would be fairly simple to establish and operate, something we could access easily from our phones and that would allow flexibility in currency and shipping. We were giving most of the socks away, so we wanted to be able to use coupon codes while still collecting mailing addresses and to set custom codes for events and conferences.

The last time Alison had been part of setting up an e-commerce site, it was 2007 and the process was a nightmare—time intensive and complicated. So when the Internet pointed us toward Shopify as a solution, she was wary. Much to her delight, the platform was a breeze to use. It was simple to set up, had lots of cool options to customize the look of the store, and was mobile friendly. By the end of the day, we had a store selling socks and she was in love.

When the @Shopify account quickly liked and replied to her tweet, the love just grew. Scott knew someone at the company, and we were invited for a visit. The whole thing had the makings of a positive brand story for the

 **Alison**
@UnAlison

I'm so madly in love with @Shopify that I think @unmarketing is relieved it's not a person ;)

LIKES
9

11:51 AM - 3 Feb 2017

UnPodcast. We'd tell the story, share our tour, give away a bunch of socks through the new site, and ride off into the brand sunset with Shopify.

However, we did not live happily ever after. This isn't that kind of story.

Alison posted the love tweet on February 3, 2017 and by the 10th the store was closed. During the first week, we started receiving tweets about Shopify's association with Breitbart News, which also was using the platform for its store, selling products like a Border Wall Construction Co. shirt. If you aren't familiar with Breitbart, some of their headlines include:

"Hoist It High and Proud: The Confederate Flag Proclaims a Glorious Heritage"

"Would You Rather Your Child Had Feminism or Cancer?"

"Gay Rights Have Made Us Dumber, It's Time to Get Back in the Closet"

Human rights advocates were using #DeleteShopify to call for a boycott of the company, and public petitions calling on Shopify to drop Breitbart were growing. One was signed by more than 20,000 people demanding the company "stop endorsing hate."

When we signed up with Shopify, we had no idea about their connection to Breitbart and their hate-filled content. We thanked everyone for bringing it to our attention and did some research of our own, including reaching out to the company to see where they stood. We found Shopify's stance on the matter even more upsetting than expected. The CEO, Tobias Lütke, had penned an open letter defending Shopify's association with Breitbart. His argument was based on defending free speech, claiming that "any attempt to apply a moral lens to what stores operate on Shopify would threaten to 'censor' a right to free expression."[1]

We were shocked and felt strongly that this was simply an excuse to continue supporting a misogynistic, anti-Semitic, and racist organization. Especially concerning for us was that the rules of "free speech" as described by Shopify do not exist in Canada, where both UnMarketing and Shopify are based. In Canada, Breitbart's content would be clearly defined as "hate speech" and would be illegal. We recognized that our own ethics and those of UnMarketing were in direct opposition to those of Shopify, and we closed our store—that day. We wrote a post on the UnMarketing Facebook page explaining why and never looked back.

The importance of ethics and working with vendors who align with your values is critical to good branding, and, we'd say, critical to humanity. We all vote with our dollars, and this applies to B2B (business-to-business) purchases as well. We didn't want our money going to a company whose values we so clearly opposed. The decision for us was simple. We'd rather go back to the 2007 e-commerce model with an ethically aligned business than work with Shopify—period.

Now our lesson here for you is not without nuance. We understand that making this kind of choice, while simple for us (with an e-commerce business that was only a tiny arm of the company we'd started less than a week earlier, with no real plans to make it revenue generating) was clear. We feel for other companies that face the decision to pull much larger, more established business in the name of ethics.

The main lesson for us is that while we were finding an e-commerce site in the first place, we should have focused more on the ethics of the company. We looked at reviews of the platform, we sought recommendations for ease of use, but we never considered searching out its political and ethical point of view. Had we done so, we never would have opened the Shopify store in the first place. Add ethics to your search parameters when looking for vendors. Seek out good companies, reward them with your dollars, and help make good values good business.

---

[1] https://techcrunch.com/2017/02/09/shopify-ceo-attempts-to-defend-continued-hosting-of-breitbarts-online-store/

Lesson 84

Burger Shop Gives Back

IN OUR DIGITAL WORLD, ONE often filled with bad news and unkindness, sometimes you need to seek out the good that people are doing. This is either to keep a positive mindset or to find ways to help or just to remind ourselves that we each can give back in our own way, even if it's only $5 at a time.

Oshawa, Ontario–based Justice Burger and its Giveback Program restores our faith in humanity. The pay-it-forward initiative encourages Justice Burger patrons to donate $5, which can then be used by future customers to pay for their food.[1] When someone gives, a coupon is pinned onto a board on the wall. People in need of food can take one of the coupons and use it to pay for their burger, no questions asked. The restaurant has had hundreds of donations, each $5 at a time, along with a few larger ones—even a check for $500 given to keep the program going.

---

[1] https://www.thestar.com/life/2017/02/24/oshawa-shop-lets-customers-buy-burgers-for-hungry-strangers.html

We love how low the barrier is for giving and how simple the process is. According to co-owner Trevor Algar, "the board, already covered in 60 pre-purchased burger coupons, is at capacity, and the $500 donation bought an additional 100 burgers for the giveback campaign. We're going to go out and get a bigger board."[2]

As brands, we don't need an excuse to give back. It shouldn't involve a campaign or a false way to create a good image. Our lesson from Justice Burger is that when giving is in the DNA of a business, it shines through and your customers will thank you for helping make the world a better place. You won't need to promote yourself as "charitable," because when you are great the world will do that for you. We ask you to look at the ways you can help your community—not just because it's good for business and not even because we've listed convergence as an important part of building loyalty. Do it simply because it's good for the world.

---

[2] http://justiceburgers.com/giveback-program/

Lesson 85

Fighting Racism Next Door

NEXTDOOR IS BRANDED AS A private social network designed to keep you up to date with what's happening in your neighborhood, "whether it's finding a last-minute babysitter, learning about an upcoming block party, or hearing about a rash of car break-ins."[1] When we first heard about the site, we were skeptical (that's our resting state really, we have resting skeptic face). First of all, for it to work you'd need your neighborhood to use it (rather than a Facebook group, for example) or old-school stuff like talking face-to-face or knowing one another's phone numbers. For an online social network to function properly, it needs users—enough users to make the communication worthwhile. Otherwise you're just standing in a virtual empty room talking to yourself.

That aside, the idea of an online neighborhood seemed like a cool idea to us. We live around other people and spend time online. We like block parties and occasionally need babysitters. The thing is, we didn't learn about Nextdoor on the App Store or because a neighbor recommended we

---

[1] https://backchannel.com/for-nextdoor-eliminating-racism-is-no-quick-fix-9305744f9c6#.fdf3ixsv7

get it going. We learned about Nextdoor by reading about how it was dealing with a very serious issue: the brand was perceived as racist.

In 2015, a story about Nextdoor claimed members were using its "crime and safety" category (one meant to share information about neighborhood concerns like theft) to target their black neighbors. It alleged that white Oakland, California, residents were using the "crime and safety" category of Nextdoor to report suspicious activity about their black neighbors. "Rather than bridging gaps between neighbors, Nextdoor can become a forum for paranoid racialism—the equivalent of the nosy Neighborhood Watch appointee in a gated community."[2] Rather than having the positive spin of a network to bring people together, the site was faced with a serious identity crisis. People will think, "Oh, Nextdoor, that's that place where people are racist."

Racism is a problem. Being perceived as a platform where racism is encouraged is a problem. Ending racism and this perception is a problem. Problem, problem, problem.

Now Nextdoor could have proceeded in a number of ways. It could have removed the category and hoped for the best or it could have focused on pushing its brand messaging to counteract the story. Many sites faced with the same issue have chosen to take no responsibility for the actions of their users. Nextdoor certainly isn't alone in this challenge. Twitter, Airbnb, and Facebook have all faced issues of racism. Nextdoor decided to go with a three-part solution.

"By the late fall of 2015, Nextdoor had landed on its initial three-part fix. First off, it put the entire neighborhood operations team through a diversity training workshop so that its members could better recognize the problem. Second, it updated the company's community guidelines and reintroduced them to its users through a blog post." Third, it added a "racial profiling" category, inviting users to report the behavior if they saw it. The problem was that many people didn't understand what it was, and Nextdoor members began reporting all kinds of unrelated slights as racial profiling.[3]

---

[2] http://fusion.net/nextdoor-the-social-network-for-neighbors-is-becoming-1793846596

[3] https://backchannel.com/for-nextdoor-eliminating-racism-is-no-quick-fix-9305744f9c6#.fdf3ixsv7

When the third part of the solution failed, Nextdoor was faced with a new challenge, and we found their answer insightful. The site's owners met with community members and engaged in difficult conversations about race, looking to the work of Jennifer Eberhardt, an expert on unconscious racial bias. The basic message of her work is that if a site made people stop and think before they posted, they probably won't do the racist things that they do. Nextdoor took this understanding and added a set of questions users had to answer before posting something to the "crime and safety" category. By making it more difficult to post, they made users stop and think before sharing. Rather than simply providing an empty field to describe a person, they made users choose from options like hair and clothing and focused reports on the event, flagging discriminatory descriptors.

These steps are important because from a social-media platform's point of view, they are counterintuitive. At UnMarketing, we have rallied behind removing steps, making sharing as seamless as possible to grow your user base. Ease of sharing encourages people to share, and more sharing grows your user base. Having more users grows your platform, and the bigger the platform, the bigger the ad dollars. We love what Nextdoor did because while it may not be the best short-term business choice, it's the best human choice, the one that will create the kind of community it was intending to build.

The lesson we took from Nextdoor is to do the work. It is far too easy to lay blame on others and avoid the effort that's needed to truly fix your company's problems. Tough challenges may call for even tougher solutions.

Lesson 86

Great Culture Has No Expiration Date

A RELATIVELY SMALL, PRIVATELY OWNED business was rated number two on *Fortune* magazine's list of the best places to work in the United States.[1] Wegmans, a 100-year-old grocery chain with headquarters in Rochester, New York, was in some pretty tough company. The top spot for the sixth year in a row went to Google, famous for its employee benefits and perks such as gourmet food and an active focus on programs that create a safe and inclusive environment for employees. Some of the reasons Wegmans earned the high rating included its inclusive domestic-partner benefits, health insurance for part-time workers, and telecommuting options for appropriate jobs. Employees related feeling that "'there's a lot of loving and caring'" in the company, where "workers have flexible schedules, ample promotion opportunities, and 'feel like family.' But it's the 'small things that make a difference,' like free cakes on birthdays and hot chocolate in the winter for anyone who works outside."

---

[1] https://www.inc.com/justin-bariso/how-a-family-owned-supermarket-chain-became-one-of-the-best-places-to-work-in-am.html

Too often, we oversimplify job satisfaction by rating it purely on compensation. However, Wegmans ranked higher than many companies that had higher-paying jobs, with many jobs in the company paying less than $11 an hour and managers earning an average salary of $60,000. We aren't sure how even base salaries at Google compare. Ninety-three percent of employees surveyed said that "management is honest and ethical in its business practices," 96% said they had "great bosses," and 97% claimed to benefit from "great communication."

One of our favorite things about Wegmans was how it demonstrates gratitude to its employees by celebrating "work anniversaries, developmental goals, and acts of service for helping others."[2] It invests in its employees through development programs, allocating more than $50 million annually in management-trainee and leadership-development programs, departmental universities, workshops, and certification programs. These are the management programs praised by 93% of the company's workforce.

In 2016, Wegmans offered $5 million in tuition assistance to both full- and part-time workers and made celebrating the recipients a community event. The CEO stated, "Customers are invited to join in a celebration at all Wegmans stores for the scholarship recipients, and all 2016 graduates, with free pieces of graduation cake at 11 A.M. on Saturday, May 21. The cake will kick off a store-wide event to introduce the summer issue of *Wegmans Menu* magazine, which includes profiles of several past scholarship recipients on pages 10 and 11."[3]

We just love everything about that. Here we see our loyalty factors at work; Wegmans focuses not only on providing cost, comfort, and convenience by actively developing a great place to work but on convergence, sharing the success of their employees with the greater community. When people feel valued, when communication is facilitated, when business practices are ethical, companies thrive. This is our Wegmans lesson: the value employees feel trickles down to front-line employees, who in turn treat customers with value and respect. Add in bringing value to your community as a whole, and we have a recipe for success.

---

[2] http://beta.fortune.com/best-companies/wegmans-food-markets-2

[3] https://www.wegmans.com/news-media/press-releases/2016/wegmans-employee-scholarship-program-reaches-record-new-recipien.htm

Lesson 87

Ethics Exchange

AS THE ONLINE WORLD HAS grown, there's been a lot of debate over how to separate personal and business worlds. We're in the "it's simply not possible to do so" camp. Everything you post, share, and endorse online reflects you personally and professionally. Whether you have a disclaimer that tweets are your own or whether you post on behalf of a company without your name attached, everything can and will be used against you. A share or retweet is an endorsement, and your name is nothing more than a LinkedIn search away. Rather than try to separate the two, we ask you to consider the things you write with care. Don't post anything you wouldn't want to see on a billboard, while driving by with your boss, your best client, and your mom in the car.

In Lesson 38, "Scott Spratten, Kitten Killer," we shared our personal branding story about *QR Codes Kill Kittens*. We hope you see the story was in fun and we actually delighted in sending out stuffed kittens to concerned children. Still, the important thing to take from it is the lack of brand boundaries between us (Scott and Alison), the *UnPodcast* (content created by us and our company), the book (also content created by us and our company), and UnMarketing (the brand). Basically, if any one of these things scares kids, they all do.

Every year during the holiday season, we see a lot of personal branding mistakes that shape our business perception of people—for example, the sharing of Facebook gift scams.

"Police are again warning folks on Facebook about the viral 'secret sister gift exchange' scam, which claims if you buy a $10 gift and send it to a 'secret sister,' you will receive anywhere from six to 36 in return. If you see this message floating around your newsfeed, you should completely ignore it and/or report it to Facebook immediately. And remember, when it comes to the Internet, if it sounds too good to be true, it usually is. But not only is the gift exchange a scam—it's also illegal. Participants receive their gifts via the mail, and pyramid schemes don't comply with United States Post Office regulations. In addition, posting personal information on Facebook (such as your address) violates the site's terms of agreement, so you also risk having your account blocked."[1]

When we see friends sharing scams like this, we can't help but judge their decision-making skills. There is no easy way to make money in the mail, and anyone who tells you there is, is making their money off you.

Share a political post, especially without comment—those are your views now. If you post a racist article, be prepared to be judged as such. Type your "LOL" at the end of a misogynistic post, and readers will guess those are your values. Everything is searchable online, and each and every action shapes your personal brand. Your employer (or future employer), your partner (or future partner), your friends, and even your children will all see these things one day. Please learn from others and share thoughtfully.

---

[1] http://www.goodhousekeeping.com/life/money/news/a35410/facebook-secret-sister-gift-exchange-scam/

Lesson 88

Too Much of a Good Thing?

AN ARTICLE IN BUSINESS NEWS DAILY recently caught our attention when it said that too many positive reviews can be bad for business. The reasoning was that the reviews set a high standard, which could be bad for business if it's not continually met, leading to customer disappointment.[1]

If you ask us, our books cannot receive too many positive reviews.

It got us thinking about reviews and whether or not we agreed with their findings. There is something to be said for the idea that some constructive negative feedback along with positive comments could make the review and reviewer seem more legitimate. For example, if we read a review about a restaurant that says the food was amazing but it was a quiet space, not really meant for a large family, that negative comment would actually be a positive if we were looking for a nice, child-free eating experience.

The issue really isn't the number of positive or negative reviews; it's the over-simplification of a 5-star rating system. Rarely can a product appeal to everyone. Rather, some people will like some things, and others will like

---

[1] http://www.businessnewsdaily.com/9295-negative-impact-good-reviews.html

other things. This can vary even day to day or hour to hour. We might give a restaurant five stars during the day for great food and a vibrant atmosphere. If we go to the very same place for dinner, the same atmosphere may be a negative, and we'd give it three stars. The restaurant hasn't changed; our wants and needs changed.

The goal should be to have as many honest reviews as possible, rewarded for detail and helpfulness so that we can read the reviews and decide if this is the right place, for the right time, for the right group. It will never be as simple as "the perfect balance is 80% positive reviews with 20% negative reviews." As a brand, how would you even control this? The worst would be for someone to read this article and then decide to treat every ninth person poorly, for optimal rating ratios.

The branding lesson here is about optimizing reviews. If you want to optimize the reviews you're getting, focus on collecting the information with as much ease as possible for your customers. We love products like Trurating,[2] which help you collect feedback at the point of sale. We love companies that reply to feedback in positive ways. If your noisy restaurant received a negative review, try commenting with an apology for the reviewer's experience and share times when the place is quieter, maybe with a coupon or another incentive to bring the customer back to try again. When feedback happens in public online spaces, most of the time people just want to be heard and have their stories validated in a helpful way. The added bonus is that onlookers will see how you reply, and they'll benefit from the information.

---

[2] https://www.trurating.com/en-ca/

Lesson 89

Work Life Balance, en Français

In our modern world, setting boundaries around work hours can be very difficult. This can be both a good thing and a challenge. For entrepreneurs, being constantly connected can allow flexibility of work hours and location. As an employee, being always at the beck and call of email and clients can come with a cost.

It's wonderful that we can work from anywhere at any time.

It's terrible that we can work from anywhere at any time.

The key to work–life balance for us is in setting sustainable expectations that we can manage. Within a company, this means open communication channels, where workers can express concerns about overtime demands and management can lay out clear expectations. These expectations should be shared with customers so that they know about wait times for responses and product and service delivery. When we know when we can expect a reply, we're much less likely to get angry about a late one.

For entrepreneurs, balance between the need for time away from work and the flexibility and constant-contact options modern technology has allowed us is essential. These needs will vary tremendously between people;

there simply is no one way to succeed at life–work balance, and anyone trying to sell you one is a crook.

In France recently, the issue of employees feeling overworked became a concern for the government. According to the *Guardian*, beginning January 1, 2017, French workers were given the "right to disconnect."[1] Under the law, companies with more than 50 employees would need to negotiate with their workforce to create boundaries around work hours and expectation.

Our lesson here isn't about which guidelines you should put into place; it's about making sure you create the right ones for you, your employees, and your market. Here are some things to consider:

- Do you or your employees find that the quality of your product and/or service is suffering because of a lack of work–life balance? If the emails you feel forced to send at 3:00 AM are lacking, you shouldn't be sending them. Respect your customers and clients enough to share your best work.

- Does your product or service demand a 24/7 mentality? While an emergency plumbing company may be obligated to provide responses on Saturday at 8:00 AM, we're pretty sure your marketing clients can wait until Monday. Decide what the product demands are, and then set them out clearly for customers.

- Is it time to hire more people? If you've decided 24/7 is your thing, you can stretch an employee pool only so far before your employees break. This isn't the time or place to save; hire more employees to lessen the load and improve the overall service you offer. You may think you're growing profits, but you're actually lowering the value of your business.

- Cut yourself some slack. Work–life balance doesn't really exist in a digital world. There is no magic equation. Spend some time deciding what's important to you, and focus on making time for that. Take the time to remember why you started that company or took that job in the first place.

---

[1] https://www.theguardian.com/money/2016/dec/31/french-workers-win-legal-right-to-avoid-checking-work-email-out-of-hours

Lesson 90

Pet-Not-So-Smart

LIFE IS GOOD FOR OUR pets. The two dogs and two cats live a spoiled life of naps, treats, and expensive spa-level packages at the kennel (Scott just can't say no). Needless to say, we're very familiar with our local pet stores and the costs involved with keeping our animals in the lifestyle they've become accustomed to.

So, when we saw this story about a PetSmart coupon gone rogue, we understood the customers' motivation. The coupon was released online without disclaimers or any digital limits on the item itself. It could be (and was) infinitely copied and used over and over. It reached people far past those it was intended for (as part of a T-Mobile offer to its customers). The coupons that were for $7 off purchases of $7 or more were soon being circulated to every Rex, Spot, and Fluffy, as they stocked up on items under $7—for free[1].

Our branding lesson here is to remember the details. Using mobile phone technology to deliver wanted discounts is very cool, and a nice way to touch

---

[1] https://consumerist.com/2016/09/20/petsmart-takes-part-in-t-mobile-tuesdays-forgets-to-limit-freebie-to-t-mobile-customers/

base with your community, partner with other businesses, and create happy customer experiences. However, not respecting just how easily these customers could also then turn around and share the unrestricted coupon was a huge thing to overlook. Please understand the technology you want to use before you use it. It's a lot easier to prevent mistakes than to clean up messes. Just ask Spot's owner in aisle 3.

Lesson 91

One Flew Over the Loyalty Nest

WHEN WE ASKED UNMARKETING FACEBOOK fans to share their stories about brand loyalty, many of them were about frustration over botched loyalty programs. As Vani Rouse wrote, sharing her AIR MILES experience,

> Been a collector since their launch. The stunt they pulled last year announcing soon-to-expire points had many people scramble to redeem from a very limited selection. They were challenged and, at the 11th hour, reversed the announcement. Great for those who were resolved to let their miles expire, bad for those who acted on the belief that our air miles were expiring.

Building brand trust takes time and effort, but breaking it can happen in one announcement. In the case of AIR MILES, it happened with two announcements. The first let customers know that their miles would expire, and the second later announced that actually, they wouldn't. The *Toronto Sun* shared a few customer stories, and one that particularly spoke to us was from 63-year-old Dolores of Sherwood Park, Alberta. "She was recently widowed after collecting AIR MILES with her late husband for over 20 years. They had saved over 17,000 points. In the past few months, she redeemed all her points because AIR MILES threatened to take them away. Dolores wrote: 'I feel very used by AIR MILES and feel that what they did is just not acceptable and that everyone that purchased goods just to use their miles up, should be redeemed those AIR MILES.'"

Dolores added, "Because of what AIR MILES has done to me, I will probably never be able to go on any more vacations. I was just so happy that I had all those miles but when I heard I had to use them, my heart was broken because that was my only way to travel."[1]

Dolores's story is unfortunately not rare; the paper was overwhelmed with similar stories.

Unless you're one of those tidy, organized folks who actually clean out their wallets, it's probably full of loyalty cards. There's that coffee shop from your vacation with its promise of a 10th free latte, the card from your local grocery store(s), the airline status card you're earned with all those miles—rewarding loyalty is big in marketing. It makes perfect sense. Businesses want loyal customers, and customers love being rewarded for loyalty. Programs can reward with free purchases, coupons, points, or credits for future purchases, extra perks to service, and sometimes access to special products, services, or information. Since referrals from happy, current customers are the best marketing tools we have, it makes sense to reward them and nurture the relationship.

Although the concept behind loyalty programs is a good one, it's important to be skeptical about whether one will work for you and whether they work in general. According to a 2015 Colloquy Customer Loyalty Census, "American households hold memberships in 29 loyalty programs spread among the retail, financial services, travel and various other economic sectors, but are active in just 12 of them."[2]

That means only one-third of loyalty programs are doing their job. For a tool that can be expensive and time consuming for a company to create and maintain, those aren't the best numbers.

---

[1] http://www.torontosun.com/2016/12/10/air-miles-needs-to-fix-the-problem-it-created

[2] https://www.colloquy.com/latest-news/2015-colloquy-loyalty-census/

Here are four of the issues we've experienced with reward programs:

1. *They don't stand out.* We counted, and between us we have 2,084 reward cards in our wallets. When most businesses are using them, you need to differentiate yours.
2. *They don't work.* This seems like a pretty obvious issue to correct, but like checking your online shopping cart, the functionality is often ignored. Focus on functionality first.
3. *They are the only reason for customers to come back.* Again, we shouldn't really need to say this, but if your product or service is lacking, no one is coming back regularly because of the promise of earning something for free.
4. *They get bogged down and become an issue for the company.* Once you've made a promise to your market, you need to keep it. Canceling programs, going back on promises, changing incentives—they all kill loyalty, and the news of your broken promise will travel.

We understand why you want loyal customers. We understand why you want them to collect and redeem rewards in a timely and controlled manner. We even understand how the good intentions of creating a loyalty program can be forgotten when you're spending more time shipping free or discounted products than full-price ones. But in the end, the only branding lesson that matters here is how the programs shape the way your customers think about you. Trust isn't a renewable resource.

Lesson 92

Gimme a Break-In

WHEN ALISON WAS PREGNANT WITH Ben, she ate one of those giant Kit Kat bars—the kind where it's just one stick and it's the size of your head—every single day. He's basically 73% Kit Kat. The chocolate bar is over 80 years old and is a brand staple with easily recognizable packaging and a well-known "gimme a break" tag line, the kind of brand we dream of creating as marketers. Because of how established it is and because it's one product within a large offering from a huge multi-national company, you may not think of it as disruptive or innovative. But you'd be wrong.

When Hunter Jobbins, a 19-year-old freshman at Kansas State University, tweeted about how someone stole a Kit Kat bar from the cup holder in his car, the brand reacted like an emerging brand.[1] Mr. Jobbins had left

---

[1] http://abc13.com/food/man-who-had-kit-kat-stolen-from-car-gets-thousands/1592773/

his car unlocked for only a few minutes, but while he was gone someone had stolen the treat and left him a note:

> Saw Kit Kat in your cup holder. I love Kit Kats so I checked your door and it was unlocked. Did not take anything other than the Kit Kat. I am sorry and hungry.

Since nothing else had been taken and no damage done, Mr. Jobbins wasn't upset about the break-in. He tweeted a photo of the note, and the post went viral. Kit Kat noticed and jumped at the opportunity to engage in a fun way with customers by sending him 6,500 Kit Kats, which were stuffed into Mr. Jobbins's Camry.

The branding lesson here is about listening for opportunities to be awesome. Every day we read that Twitter is dead or about the next big place online we need to be. We bend over backward for angry customers, field negative reviews, and put valuable time into pushing our messages out into the world in the name of new-customer acquisition, leaving very little room to return the high-fives of happy customers and find opportunities like this one to do cool things. If you reply only to angry comments, you're leaving your fans hanging and missing the chance to create stories that spread.

Lesson 93

Stone-Cold Success

Two summers ago, we were sitting outside the house letting our kids dump ice water over our heads and recording it—all in the name of the ALS Ice Bucket Challenge. It was a social-media phenomenon, shared prolifically and impossible to avoid. The challenge quickly became a case study for charitable organizations seeking funds and awareness. We wrote about it in Chapter 26, "Social Media for Social Good" in the second edition of *UnMarketing*. A perfect storm of video-enabled phones, social-media platforms, a worthy cause, a well-established organization, and a simple directive created one of the most successful fundraising campaigns in history.

The challenge raised a ton of money, flooding the organization with unprecedented resources. After the fad died down, we have been impressed not only with how the organization has continued to use the money for good but how it's kept the world informed about where the money went. As we saw with Charity Water in Lesson 63, "The Thirst for Good Branding," supplying social proof and connection is one of the most important tools digital innovations offer. The ALS Association (ALSA) provided transparency and released information showing where the Ice Bucket Challenge money went:

- $115 million total were raised.
- 67% (77 million) went to funding research.
- 20% (23 million) went to provide patient and community resources.
- 9% (10 million) went to public and professional education.
- 2% (2.5 million) went to continued fund-raising campaigns.
- 2% (2.5 million) went to external processing fees.[1]

Under the research umbrella, ALSA recently announced the discovery of NEK1, "which scientists say is among the most common genes that contribute to the disease [amyotrophic lateral sclerosis] and is associated with 3 percent of A.L.S. cases. The discovery, published in *Nature Genetics*, is the result of a global gene-sequencing effort involving 11 countries and 80 researchers, called Project MinE."[2]

Also this year, the U.S. Food and Drug Administration approved the first new drug for the treatment of ALS in more than two decades. To support research and to support the efforts that led to these discoveries, funds were used to set up a number of grants and awards to support researchers and innovation, local support chapters for ALS sufferers, and greater access to support and education materials for those living with the disease.[3]

There is a lot of cynicism about charitable giving online. When the Ice Bucket Challenge was in full swing, many termed it "slacktivism"—actions performed via the Internet in support of a political or social cause but regarded as requiring little time or involvement (e.g., signing an online petition or joining a campaign group on a social-media website). We know one can't equate dropping a bucket of ice on your head with dedicating your life to research. We know liking or sharing a photo of a child in need isn't the same thing as donating time, energy, and resources to the child.

[1] http://www.alsa.org/fight-als/ibc-infographic.html

[2] https://www.nytimes.com/2016/07/28/health/the-ice-bucket-challenge-helped-scientists-discover-a-new-gene-tied-to-als.html

[3] http://www.cnn.com/2017/05/06/health/new-als-drug/index.html

But when you see the power of large groups of people doing small things together in the name of good, it's tough to downplay the possibilities of social media for social good—and that's the lesson for us from the Ice Bucket Challenge. Put your cynicism and doubt aside in the name of kindness and doing good. Do something, whatever you can—whether it's a like, a share, or a donation of your dollars or time. Don't let feeling like you can't do everything get in the way of doing something, because a lot of little somethings can add up.

Lesson 94

Charming Pretend Lines

LAST YEAR FOR HER BIRTHDAY, Tessa got a Pandora bracelet and a few charms. She loves it, and with a store in our local mall, Pandora quickly became a regular place to browse when we were running errands. Over time, the bracelet had become a little dirty (10-year-olds are entitled to messy bracelets), so we stopped in before the holidays to see if we could get it cleaned and also to see which charms Tessa liked so we could add one to her Chanukah present.

On stop number one, we were told they offered free cleanings for all jewelry but wouldn't be doing them during weekend hours, so we'd need to come back on a weekday. Although the store wasn't very busy, we understood and didn't mind the stop since we were in the mall anyway. Tessa showed Alison a pretty menorah charm she wanted for Chanukah, so it was still a pretty successful trip.

On stop two, Alison went in on a weekday morning and was told they wouldn't be doing cleanings because they had a special promotion on that day. She asked if she could leave the bracelet for cleaning and they said she could not. Although once again the store wasn't busy, Alison wasn't too upset because it gave her a chance to buy the charm for Tessa. Two stops and Pandora was still getting our business—she didn't even complain on social media! See, we can be reasonable!

On stop three, on a weekday afternoon without a promotion, Alison tried to go into Pandora and was stopped at the door by an employee who asked her to wait in line before entering. There wasn't a line at the time, just some ropes one might use to organize a line—and Alison. The employee told her that she needed to wait until one of the employees inside was free; then she could go in. While she waited a line formed behind her, after each shopper was told to wait and was offered a brochure to look at. After a few minutes, Alison was let in, and she approached one of the salespeople. She asked if she could have Tessa's bracelet cleaned to which the employee replied, "Which kind of bracelet do you have?" This was a question no other employee had previously asked on any of the visits.

"It's a blue leather band with four charms."

"Oh, we don't clean those. Only the silver and gold jewelry can be cleaned."

As you can image, Alison would have appreciated this information on trips one through three.

Three trips, one new charm, and one fake line later Alison was done. She'd been in the store three times and was told she had to wait, she kept coming back because none of the staff took the time to really find out why she was there, and we'd spent money on a new charm and had been a part of a fake line to draw attention to a promotion. The brand lesson here is to keep your front-line motivated for ways to say yes. When customers come into your location, they are looking for help. If your employees' instinct is always to find a way out of helping, your customers will be left feeling unheard and unhappy.

Lesson 95

The Stench of Going Above and Beyond

WE LOVE WHEN COMPANIES GO that extra mile. We've written about that in all five of our books and speak about it on the *UnPodcast* every week and from the stage during keynotes. It's rare, wonderful, and sadly newsworthy. All too often what we consider "above and beyond" is simply companies keeping their promises. Alison actually all-caps freaked out recently when Amazon.ca found a lost shipment she'd ordered and had it sent out again at no extra charge. Imagine, they found AND fixed the problem, all over chat! She didn't even need to get on the phone. Above and beyond!

And then sometimes, it gets awkward.

We needed a plumber. A pipe was leaking through the ceiling of one of the kids' bedrooms, and anything beyond looking up and saying, "yep, it's leaking" goes way above our pay grade. We went online to Homestars.com, a service-provider–review site (like a Yelp/Angie's List for Canadians). We researched a few plumbers, read the reviews of complete strangers (who we hoped weren't also serial killers or had bad taste in plumbers). We trusted their opinions, and chose a plumber to try, whom we're going to call Jeff.

Jeff showed up on time, did the work we asked for, and gave us a little bit of extra time and help with some ideas to prevent more leaks in the future. He was tidy and polite. We were both happy with the whole experience. Now, we aren't saying we invited Jeff for dinner and asked him to join our Fantasy Football League, but we were satisfied with the plumbing services he provided. We met on the front porch to take care of payment and take his business card, when he decided to add a little something extra:

"You know, I really went above and beyond today!"

There are things you should say about yourself, and then there are things you should reserve for other people to say to you, and this was one of them. We love that Jeff is proud of his work. He should totally go home and tell his partner and kids and even himself in the mirror that he "went above and beyond today." Pride is important, and most of us are way too hard on ourselves. But telling a customer you went above and beyond when clearly you have simply done your job—the one we were about to pay you for—was just creepy. It sounded a lot like asking for an extra big tip. When you're good, you tell people. When you're great, other people say it for you. It's like when people call themselves leaders; that is a title given to you by others, not something to be self-proclaimed to those you're trying to lead.

Scott was taken aback. He replied the way he would to a child proudly showing off their new shoe-tying skills on their brand-new Velcro shoes.

"Well, good for you, Jeff."

Jeff didn't take the hint, and he went on:

"We're number one on Homestars. We always get 5-star reviews."

Scott handed Jeff his money and walked inside with a scrunched brow, trying to figure out what had just happened. It seemed Jeff Proudy-Pants believed a job well done was "above and beyond." He made it weird.

Here are some branding lessons from Jeff:

1. Focus on doing a good job, and the reviews will come.
2. If you choose to ask for reviews (which is something we suggest you do) make sure you aren't putting people on the spot. If Jeff wanted to make sure we thought he'd provided great service, he could have asked if there was anything else he could do or asked if we were happy with all the work he'd done.

3. Jeff had our contact information, so he had a less "in our face" option for asking for reviews. He could have written a nice follow-up letter to make sure we were happy and provided a link to leave a review—easy-peasy, with 82% less awkwardness.

We want to recognize that it's entirely possible none of this is Jeff's fault. He may be under pressure from his boss, who rewards reviews with much-needed bonus work or pay. Jeff might also lose future jobs if he isn't getting customers to leave reviews for the company. His boss probably read some business book from a social-media expert who told him reviews were important and the key to success in the age of disruption.

All we know is that we haven't called Jeff since. We called a different plumber recently, and he did the job just right—just ask him.

Lesson 96

United We Fall

WE COULD WRITE AT LEAST a dozen books about airlines, about how they mess up and how they impress us—so many stories, so little time. For *UnBranding*, we've decided to focus on United Airlines. They've really left us no choice, as time and time and time again this past year they have left us saying "this must be the worst thing an airline could do to its customers!"

First, we have their pricing tiers, to which they recently added Basic Economy. Should you find yourself in one of these seats—the least expensive seats now available—you will be allowed only one personal item, and it must fit under the seat. They've removed the previous "luxury" item—access to the overhead bin. They've also removed the ability to chose seats from Basic, meaning that travelers flying together will most likely find themselves separated, with higher-fare-paying customers having access to seats first.[1]

"This has to be the worst thing an airline could do to its customers," said Scott.

---

[1] http://www.denverpost.com/2016/12/06/united-airlines-charging-to-use-overhead-bins/

Then came the leggings scandal. Two girls were denied boarding on a United flight because they were traveling on a "friends and family" pass, and according to the airline's dress code rules for such passengers, leggings were not acceptable. The list of unacceptable dress includes ""swimwear, see-through clothing, flip flops, slippers, anything with holes or tears, and anything that reveals your midriff or undergarments and form-fitting Lycra or spandex pants, such as leggings."

The incident was documented by Shannon Watts,[2] an activist and fellow passenger, who shared the experience online. Social media outrage ensued and included this gem from Delta.

 **Delta** ✓
@Delta

 Following ⌄

Flying Delta means comfort. (That means you can wear your leggings. 😉)

RETWEETS   LIKES
32,060   120,001

We were sent the story by countless UnMarketing fans, friends, and other parents, all outraged over the gate-agent treatment of the children and United's policy. Our concerns included:

1. The policy is outdated and doesn't take into account casual dress of our time (which certainly includes leggings).
2. The policy is open to a wide range of interpretation, leaving it open to discrimination and sexism. We travel extensively and regularly see all forms of this list walking on and off planes. It is up to the gate agent to make the call on whom to stop and whom to let through.
3. The policy is disrespectful. These were children, and the act of saying their clothing is inappropriate because it is tight sexualizes them.

---

[2] http://www.nbcnews.com/news/us-news/united-airlines-leggings-incident-shows-changing-nature-air-travel-n738926

4. The policy is useless. From a branding perspective, other travelers cannot tell who is on a friends and family pass and who is not, so the distinction means nothing to the general public.

"This has to be the worst thing an airline could do to its customers." said Alison.

Most recently, we had the re-accommodation scandal. After everyone had taken their seats on a United flight from Chicago to Louisville, four staff members arrived at the gate and the airline decided they needed to be seated on the flight, meaning four already boarded customers would need to give up their seats. This was opportunity number one for United to make a respectful choice. With the destination only a four-hour drive away, United could have paid to have these employees drive (or be driven) to their stop. But they didn't.

An announcement was made and passengers were offered money to give up their seats. They went as high as offering $800. This was opportunity number two for United to make a respectful choice. It could and should have offered much more for this seat exchange, but it chose to stop well below that amount.

Dr. David Dao and his wife initially volunteered to leave, but when they learned the next option to get them home was too late for them, they sat back down and explained that Dr. Dao had patients waiting for him so they couldn't go. Airplane staff decided this was unacceptable and insisted he leave. Things escalated from there. This was opportunity number three for United to do the respectful thing: let Dr. Dao and his wife remain and continue to seek out others to deplane.

Moments later, Dr. Dao was being dragged violently down the aisle, hitting his head on an armrest, as the rest of the passengers looked on. Several passengers filmed the incident and shared their videos online. The staff followed protocol for an incident when a passenger refuses to get off a flight and called in local law enforcement to do the job. This represented opportunities number four through 101 for United to make a respectful choice. This did not need to escalate to violence—violence that injured and traumatized a man, along with everyone else on the flight.

When news of the incident hit social media, United came under fire. United's CEO, Oscar Munoz, proceeded to release a statement blaming the victim and defending his employees' actions. Mr. Munoz described the violent removal as an effort to "re-accommodate" passengers. This was opportunity number 102 for United to make a respectful choice, apologize in a heartfelt manner, and promise to make amends and changes going forward.[3]

United's stocks nosedived, and the company's value initially decreased by approximately $1 billion. Mr. Munoz then released a second apology. Accusations of racism and profiling were made against the airline for targeting Dr. Dao.[4] This was opportunity number 103 for United to make a respectable choice. A second apology after losing a lot of money is both too little and way too late. It's clearly disingenuous and empty.

"Please, for the love of all that is holy, let this be the worst thing an airline could do to its customers," said the world.

The day after the incident, in an unprecedented emergency recording of the *UnPodcast*, we spoke to Dave Carroll, the creator of the viral hit "United Breaks Guitars." Here are some of the gems Dave had to share about United:

> Like a lot of people, I think you watch that video and put yourself in the shoes of the passengers on that plane, and I thought, "If I was with my kids on that plane, how would they be reacting to seeing what looked like the bouncers from *Roadhouse* ripping in and taking somebody out of their seat?" I felt for the guy obviously, and I think that anytime your passengers are being taken out of a plane in a semi-conscious state, that you're having a bad day.
>
> This is serious business, and not just because things got physical on a plane. It speaks to what I like to think of as a lack of compassion that's in big companies, and United is just a metaphor for this sort of thing.

---

[3] http://www.cnn.com/2017/04/11/travel/united-customer-dragged-off-overbooked-flight/index.html

[4] https://www.theguardian.com/us-news/2017/apr/11/united-airlines-shares-plummet-passenger-removal-controversy

That if a culture of compassion was present in the airline, then the way people would treat their customers, or their suppliers or other employees on a daily basis would be radically different than what happened on that plane.

It's not just about the dollars and cents, and that's what the problem with big companies are, they focus on shareholder value, or how much profit did we make and they don't realize the damage they're doing with their branding. So they could have a plane full of people, Southwest could have a plane full and United could have an exact same size aircraft full of people and when they get off on the other end the conversations everybody's going to have may be radically different, and both may make the same money but the damage to the brand—in this case it would be United—is going to filter down and it's going to affect how the customers are looking at and treating the employees and maybe vice versa. This ill will spreads like a virus throughout the organization. After "United Breaks Guitars" went viral, early on, I received two independent letters from the flight attendants and the pilots on their own letterhead, their association letterheads, and I'm paraphrasing, but essentially they said, if you think it's bad flying with us, try working here. How can you impress and dazzle your customers when the people delivering the services have no faith in the organization?

They dropped the ball in so many ways, and they have such an us-and-them culture. I think that's the problem.

They could change things. They could become a more compassionate company and create a complete culture change, but it's not going to happen overnight and they have to have a will to do it.

Westjet has those great ads, that tug at your heartstrings. But if United had tried to do that it wouldn't have worked because their story is not congruent with that—Westjet's is.[5]

Here's the lesson we can learn from United: when you focus only on the bottom line and treat your employees poorly, you create a culture of disrespect that becomes synonymous with your brand. The incident on the plane wasn't an isolated event, it was congruent with the brand. As Dave said so well, "If a culture of compassion was present in the airline, then the way people would treat their customers, or their suppliers or other employees on a daily basis would be radically different than what happened on that plane." Learn from United and actively create a culture of compassion; it's good business and good branding.

Lesson 97

Hook-and-Ladder Stratten

WE WERE IN ORLANDO, FLORIDA for a conference, escaping the humidity with a trip to one of the city's amazing and, thankfully, air-conditioned malls, when Scott decided lunch should involve a little research. He'd recently booked a keynote presentation with Firehouse Subs—a U.S. chain of casual restaurants known for its steamed subs. At the time, Firehouse didn't have any locations in Canada, so Scott had never tried them, and this just couldn't stand. One simply doesn't get up onstage in front of hundreds of sub experts without personal experience, and he was hungry.

It was love at first bite. In fact, if Scott ever was to look at a woman the way he looks at a Smokehouse Brisket and Cheddar sub from Firehouse, there would be a problem.

Since that lunch, Firehouse has become a staple on the road. Whenever we see one, we go—every time. A few months ago, Firehouse opened its first location in our neighborhood, and it now has a bunch in Canada. Our oldest child just got a job at the location near his college, and our next-oldest has already applied for a summer job at the local spot. They're lucky Scott hasn't changed their names legally to Hook and Ladder.

Along with their food, preparing for the keynote also had us falling in love with the brand. Firehouse was created by brothers and former firefighters Chris and Robin Sorensen in Jacksonville, Florida.[1] Their family, including their father, can trace their participation in fire and police service back at least 200 years. Combining their personal experience, entrepreneurial spirit, and history of service, the brothers developed the idea for Firehouse—scribbling the beginnings of the franchise on a napkin while sitting in the parking lot of a soon-to-be competitor's restaurant.

In today's social-media world, franchises often struggle with identity issues. Customers see the company as one unified brand, with each location and voice continuously affecting brand perception. This becomes problematic when one good—or bad—franchise experience ends up affecting all locations across the board. To maintain brand unity, Firehouse keeps strict control over each location's look, feel, quality, and customer-service expectations. It does this by carefully managing growth. As Robin has said, "We could easily have two or three thousand stores by now. Grow too fast, and you can feel the rivets coming out of the wings."

To control growth, there is a stringent process for vetting would-be owners. CEO Don Fox cites Firehouse Subs' "diligent franchisee screening process as its biggest differentiator in the industry. No franchisee is hired without interviewing with Fox, the founders, and the CFO. From there, the candidate must spend at least one week with an area representative in an effort to better understand if the opportunity is a career fit."[2] All businesses looking to franchise should be following their lead.

The company is also debt free, frugal, and focused on providing as much value to the customer as possible, with an emphasis on using local products. During the 2009 recession, the brothers decided to increase radio advertising rather than shy away from it. This was a risk that paid off, and franchisees continued to see strong sales.

Along with maintaining the quality of each location, Firehouse is committed to consistency in each restaurant's commitment to the

---

[1] http://southernjournalmagazine.com/feature-story-look-firehouse-subs/

[2] https://www.qsrmagazine.com/exclusives/how-firehouse-subs-got-1000-units

community. The nonprofit they founded in 2005, the Firehouse Subs Public Safety Foundation,[3] has raised more than $4 million, most of which it distributes directly to public-service organizations. Each location supports local fire and safety organizations, and the commitment to do so is listed among factors such as owner credit score and investment when franchisees sign on.

This is the kind of dedication to brand unity we all can learn from. Whether you are part of a franchise, an entrepreneur, or part of a company, we can all learn from the attention to detail Chris and Robin Sorensen have been able to maintain. Growth is a good thing only when it's managed and controlled and when you have the resources to maintain it. Each location, each point of contact with your market, is an opportunity—but it is also a risk. If the spot we'd had our first Firehouse meal had been sub-par, if the community service message had been weak or nonexistent, if the teenager working the cash register had been rude or distracted, if the brisket had been cold, this might have been a different story. As we discussed when we looked at loyalty-creating factors, consistency creates comfort, and there's no business teaching a better lesson in consistency than Firehouse Subs.

[3] https://www.entrepreneur.com/article/223036

Lesson 98

The "All-Natural" Lawsuit

YOU DON'T NEED TO BE a current customer to have a feeling about a brand. Your company's good works can bring in new customers, improve your current customers' experiences with you, and create shareable brand stories. On the other hand, unethical practices will have the opposite effect, not only on your market (current and prospective) but on your ability to retain and hire successful employees. When we discuss ethics, we don't mean that every business should be saving the world or joining hands to sing kumbaya. In short, treat people with respect, follow through with your promises, and be honest about the products you make.

The dietary-supplement industry is enormous. According to Forbes.com, in 2012 the nutritional-supplement industry produced about $32 billion in revenue with no sign of slowing down. Furthermore, it is projected to double that by topping $60 billion in 2021, according to the *Nutritional Business Journal*."[1]

---

[1] https://www.forbes.com/sites/davidlariviere/2013/04/18/nutritional-supplements-flexing-their-muscles-as-growth-industry/#40a45c5f8845

Anyone with an Instagram or Snapchat account or who opens a magazine or turns on the TV can see that supplements are everywhere. As a society, we seem addicted to the idea that there's a secret pill, or tea, or powder that will provide a shortcut to health and well-being. You may be asking yourself what the harm is. If the new detox tea or vitamin helps you to be fit, then so be it. Hand over your money for the magic beans, and see what happens.

The problem is that unlike other health products, "makers of dietary supplements are not required to demonstrate that their products are safe or effective."[2] Even if you're willing to overlook proof of effectiveness, you should not ignore the lack of safety. Thankfully for all of us, there are independent researchers who make it their focus to provide checks and balances for the public. One of them is Dr. Pieter Cohen, a researcher and industry watchdog who has been looking into dietary supplements and so-called all natural ingredients for years. It came to Dr. Cohen and his team's attention that the U.S. Food and Drug Administration (FDA) had found a dangerous chemical in nine all-natural supplements. Although the FDA did not report the supplement names publically, Dr. Cohen's team replicated the studies and was able to identify the brands that in some cases had dangerously high levels of this chemical.

One of the named companies, Hi-Tech, filed a lawsuit against Dr. Cohen[3] and three of his co-authors for $200 million, because the study led to a loss of revenue. In the end, a jury ruled in favor of Dr. Cohen and dismissed the charges. We find our lesson in something Dr. Cohen said about the lawsuit, explaining that his "experience has really reinforced to me why it is so important to not only continue the research we're doing but to be very aggressive about speaking out about it."

Protect good practices, speak out about wrongdoing, be on the right side of history. In the short run, there may be challenges, but in the long run all the hard work and challenges will be worth it.

---

[2] https://consumerist.com/2017/02/08/a-supplement-company-sued-over-research-it-didnt-like-and-lost/?utm_source=facebook&utm_medium=socialflow

[3] https://consumerist.com/2017/02/08/a-supplement-company-sued-over-research-it-didnt-like-and-lost/

Lesson 99

Brand Values
Are Cool

FEW COMPANIES HAVE BEEN MORE disruptive to the way we used to get things done than Amazon. It's changed the way we shop and sell, the way we search, the way we give gifts, and even the way we support causes we care about. Our moms even buy things on Amazon. As authors, Amazon changed the way we thought of best-seller status, brought reviews to the forefront, and changed publishing. It set a new standard for shipping with same-day services and free options. This year we bought all our children's school supplies on Amazon and ran an entire holiday gift-giving extravaganza called UnSecret Santa using wish lists.

According to Bloomberg, Amazon has become the first place many people go to search for products, with more than half of U.S. online consumers beginning their product searches on Amazon.com or the mobile app.[1] Reviews drive the ecosystem. They facilitate online shopping, helping people over the trust gap created when we buy things we haven't seen in person. The site has continually prohibited and cracked down on

---

[1] https://www.bloomberg.com/news/articles/2016-09-27/more-than-50-of-shoppers-turn-first-to-amazon-in-product-search

incentivized reviews to maintain the trust of their shoppers—even going so far as to sue businesses who pay for fake reviews, as well as the individuals who write them.[2] Just when we thought Amazon was done, they unveiled a new initiative for in-store shopping with Amazon Go.[3] Even in the world of brick-and-mortar, Amazon was thinking differently. Customers at their stores don't need to wait in line or go through traditional checkouts (there are no cashiers); one simply walks through the store making choices, which are tracked using the Amazon Go app, and charges are put through when you walk out.

In *The Everything Store*, a book about Amazon founder Jeff Bezos by Brad Stone, the author shares a list made by Bezos at a point where he was reevaluating company values. The list demonstrates Bezos taking stock of his company's strengths and weaknesses, and comparing these to the qualities he admired in other companies:

Rudeness is not cool. Defeating tiny guys is not cool. Close-following is not cool. Young is cool. Risk taking is cool. Winning is cool. Polite is cool. Defeating bigger, unsympathetic guys is cool. Inventing is cool. Explorers are cool. Conquerors are not cool. Obsessing over competitors is not cool. Empowering others is cool. Capturing all the value only for the company is not cool. Leadership is cool. Conviction is cool. Straightforwardness is cool. Pandering to the crowd is not cool. Hypocrisy is not cool. Authenticity is cool. Thinking big is cool. The unexpected is cool. Missionaries are cool. Mercenaries are not cool."[4]

We love this list. We can learn a lot from how Mr. Bezos pays attention to the values driving Amazon's decision making. These ideas shape each and every choice we make in business. Revisit your values list often, because branding is about taking big ideas and using them to shape day-to-day interactions with purpose.

---

[2] https://techcrunch.com/2016/10/03/amazon-bans-incentivized-reviews-tied-to-free-or-discounted-products/

[3] http://mashable.com/2016/12/05/amazon-go-shopping/

[4] https://www.amazon.com/The-Everything-Store-Bezos-Amazon-ebook/dp/B00BWQW73E?tag=bisafetynet2-20

One of the less-than-successful products to come out of Amazon was its Fire Phone. When asked about the product, and others that have failed, Mr. Bezos' response is legendary. "If you think that's a big failure, we're working on much bigger failures right now. And I am not kidding. And some of them are going to make the Fire Phone look like a tiny little blip." He went on to say, "The size of your mistakes needs to grow along with the company. If it doesn't, you're not going to be inventing at scale that can actually move the needle. And to do so, you need to make 'big, noticeable' mistakes."[5]

We stood up and slow-clapped when we read that. Don't be afraid of failure. Take a lesson from Amazon: to make big changes, to innovate, and to thrive during times of innovation, you need to be willing to take risks.

---

[5] http://www.businessinsider.de/jeff-bezos-why-fire-phone-was-a-good-thing-2016-5

Lesson 100

Isn't *Yelp* the Sound a Dog Makes When It's in Distress?

ONLINE REVIEWS ARE ONE OF the most disruptive tools in marketing today. Their value cannot be understated. While many companies have focused on creating great experiences and products to generate positive reviews, some have decided to focus their energy and attention defensively as they publically battle, dispute, and defend.

At UnMarketing, our top three most-asked questions are:

1. What's the next big thing in social media and digital marketing? (In other words, are Twitter, Snapchat, YouTube, etc., dead?)
2. Scott, I also want a man-bun; what's your secret to great hair?
3. What can we do about negative reviews online?

If you're spending your days stressing over a pile of negative Yelp reviews, we're here to inform you: You don't have a Yelp problem. You don't have a social-media problem. What you do have is a business problem. Improve your product or service and reviews will improve. If years ago we had offered you a service that would let you listen to and analyze reviews, you'd have paid us a $1 million to access it. But now that it's here and available you want us to silence it. Stop it!

You get one angry, causeless review from a client—shame on them. You get 20, 50, or 100 and bury your head in the sand—shame on you.

When a couple in Texas were unhappy with the service they received from a pet-sitting company they'd hired to look after their pets (two dogs and a fish) while on vacation, they went on Yelp and shared their 1-star story.[1] The review was thorough, listing issues with communication, payment, and the care of their beloved fish: "We have a camera on the bowl, and we watched the water go from clear to cloudy."

Here are some things the pet sitters could have done:

1. *Ignore the review.* We don't recommend this, but it would have been better than what ended up happening. Because reviews are public, ignoring your customers also becomes public. Most of the time people just want to be heard. Your silence shows them and anyone else reading the review that you simply don't care.

2. *Reply with an apology.* Show the customer you care about his or her experience. Acknowledge what happened and say you're sorry. Check your reply for defensiveness and excuses and for blame targeted at the customer. The negative review can be an opportunity to come out looking even better than you did before it happened. Remember, publicized customer service not only helps the individual reviewer, but exponentially reaches everyone reading the review. Consider adding an offer to make things right.

3. *Respond angrily and defensively.* Follow this up with a cease-and-desist notice directing the customers to remove their review. When they don't, file a lawsuit for around $6,700 and accuse the couple of violating a non-disparagement clause in their customer agreement. When the original complaint hits the news and goes viral, drop the complaint and refile one for $1 million and include defamation charges.

---

[1] https://www.yelp.com/biz/prestigious-pets-dallas

Yeah, they went with that third option.

In the end the judge dealing with the case dismissed the charges. Just think of how many improvements to their business the pet sitters could have made if they'd redirected all that energy, time, and money onto their business rather than on lawyers and the court case. Our lesson here is to manage negative reviews with respect and respond to them publicly and quickly so your market can see that you're listening. See negative reviews as an opportunity rather than a curse.

Conclusion

TOGETHER, WE'VE LOOKED AT 100 brand lessons.

We've learned how to create comfort through consistency and how great service leads to high perceived value. We've learned the value of truth in advertising and how false advertising ends up making our real product look twice as bad because brand trust isn't a renewable resource.

We've learned that social media provides a megaphone for whatever is good or bad in our business, whether we're an established company or a scrappy Kickstarter campaign just getting off the ground. If our products are failing, exploding, or never even making it into production, we are ready to focus on those issues first.

We've learned how to make tough decisions and lead our companies as though we'll be in business for 100 years. We're ready to be leaders who serve and who value and facilitate community. We know how to build brands that have giving in their DNA and to use digital innovations to connect people over shared, authentic stories for good.

We've learned the trickle-down effect of valuing our workforce and treating employees with respect, because we know the best way to improve our bottom line is by improving our front line. As leaders and entrepreneurs, we are prepared to focus on building our strengths and outsourcing our weaknesses. We've learned the importance of creating the right boundaries for work–life balance for ourselves and our employees and of building productive teams by facilitating communication—with a little fun on the side. We've learned that saying no is the best way to make room for more of what we want to say yes to.

We've learned that convenience matters. We are ready to give our customers as many logical ways to consume content as possible while making them jump through as few hoops as possible to buy from us and connect with us.

We've learned that reviews and feedback represent opportunities, and we've learned how to optimize our brand chances for positive, authentic, honest reviews. We won't forget to return the high-fives of our happy customers, and we'll listen to and respect the views of our market, no matter how small.

We've learned to ask why and focus on the innovations our customers need, not just the ones we want to use. We won't be part of breaking the integrity of the very platforms that have brought us success and word of mouth. We've learned not to use a platform, a new technology, or a joke to appear cool or cutting edge. Our only answer to "Why?" will never be "Because that's what our competition is doing" or "Because that's how we've always done it." We won't out-innovate our customers or jump away from our tried-and-true in the name of new and shiny.

We've learned the importance of well-gotten data and asking the right questions. We'll take this data and use it to make informed decisions.

We won't mail in our content or use the content of others without credit and permission. We will disclose. We won't do lazy branding; we'll pay attention to the details, we'll put in the effort, and we won't trick people into clicking or buying. We've learned to audit our ethics and our business practices.

We're going to go out into the brand world and speak up when we see wrongdoing and injustice. We will be consumer advocates, and we won't let our brand values get dusty on our office walls. We are ready to value congruence and will revisit our values often. We'll adapt to change, put values at the center of our actions, and be on the right side of history.

We have learned that creating loyalty is the best defense against fast-paced change in the age of disruption. We know we can build loyalty by focusing on ways to create comfort, high perceived value, convenience, and congruence for our customers and our would-be market.

We've learned. And now we're ready to do the work of building and growing a brand we can be proud of, a brand deserving of loyal customers who will chose our brands habitually, share their positive brand stories, defend our brand when needed, and be impermeable to competition, no matter what innovation may bring.

Thank you for learning with us. If you've enjoyed the trip and want to join us for more, you can find us at www.UnMarketing.com, on the UnMarketing Facebook page, or on Twitter, where you can find Scott (@UnMarketing) and Alison (@unalison) always happy to chat. If you love brand stories, listen to the *UnPodcast*, where we talk weekly about business news stories, innovations, consumer advocacy, and the brands we love or love to hate. On the show we have weekly features where we answer fan questions and have some fun with made-up words. If you'd like Jackass Whisperer Socks or a mug, join us and submit a question or word. If email is your thing, you can send us your feedback, comments, questions, and random stuff to unbranding@unmarketing.com

If you'd like to read more, we have four other books to chose from: *UnMarketing: Everything Has Changed and Nothing Is Different*; *The Book of Business Awesome/UnAwesome*; *UnSelling: The New Customer Experience*; and *QR Codes Kill Kittens*. While Alison is happiest behind her laptop writing, Scott's brilliance truly shines onstage. If you're looking for energy, passion, knowledge, and humor to make your conference unmissable, learn more about bringing Scott to keynote your event at http://www.ScottStratten.com

Index